The Complete Idiot's Guide® to Facebook®

The Complete Idiot's Guide® to Facebook®

by Joe Kraynak and Mikal E. Belicove

ALPHA

A member of Penguin Group (USA) Inc.

ALPHA BOOKS

Published by the Penguin Group

Penguin Group (USA) Inc., 375 Hudson Street, New York, New York 10014, USA

Penguin Group (Canada), 90 Eglinton Avenue East, Suite 700, Toronto, Ontario M4P 2Y3, Canada (a division of Pearson Penguin Canada Inc.)

Penguin Books Ltd., 80 Strand, London WC2R 0RL, England

Penguin Ireland, 25 St. Stephen's Green, Dublin 2, Ireland (a division of Penguin Books Ltd.)

Penguin Group (Australia), 250 Camberwell Road, Camberwell, Victoria 3124, Australia (a division of Pearson Australia Group Pty. Ltd.)

Penguin Books India Pvt. Ltd., 11 Community Centre, Panchsheel Park, New Delhi—110 017, India

Penguin Group (NZ), 67 Apollo Drive, Rosedale, North Shore, Auckland 1311, New Zealand (a division of Pearson New Zealand Ltd.)

Penguin Books (South Africa) (Pty.) Ltd., 24 Sturdee Avenue, Rosebank, Johannesburg 2196, South Africa

Penguin Books Ltd., Registered Offices: 80 Strand, London WC2R 0RL, England

Copyright © 2010 by Joe Kraynak and Mikal E. Belicove

International Standard Book Number: 978-1-61564-036-2
Library of Congress Catalog Card Number: 2009943486

12   11   10   8   7   6   5   4   3   2   1

Interpretation of the printing code: The rightmost number of the first series of numbers is the year of the book's printing; the rightmost number of the second series of numbers is the number of the book's printing. For example, a printing code of 10-1 shows that the first printing occurred in 2010.

Printed in the United States of America

Note: This publication contains the opinions and ideas of its authors. It is intended to provide helpful and informative material on the subject matter covered. It is sold with the understanding that the authors and publisher are not engaged in rendering professional services in the book. If the reader requires personal assistance or advice, a competent professional should be consulted.

The authors and publisher specifically disclaim any responsibility for any liability, loss, or risk, personal or otherwise, which is incurred as a consequence, directly or indirectly, of the use and application of any of the contents of this book.

Most Alpha books are available at special quantity discounts for bulk purchases for sales promotions, premiums, fund-raising, or educational use. Special books, or book excerpts, can also be created to fit specific needs.

For details, write: Special Markets, Alpha Books, 375 Hudson Street, New York, NY 10014.

Publisher: *Marie Butler-Knight*

Associate Publisher: *Mike Sanders*

Senior Managing Editor: *Billy Fields*

Acquisitions Editor: *Tom Stevens*

Senior Development Editor: *Phil Kitchel*

Senior Production Editor: *Megan Douglass*

Copy Editor: *Jaime Julian Wagner*

Cover Designer: *Rebecca Batchelor*

Book Designers: *William Thomas, Rebecca Batchelor*

Indexer: *Brad Herriman*

Layout: *Brian Massey*

Proofreader: *Laura Caddell*

From Joe: *To Facebook users worldwide, who make Facebook the most intriguing digital hangout on the planet.*

From Mikal: *To my 75-year-old Mother, Glenda Belicove, who taught me everything I ever needed to know about living an authentic life, as well as a few things about using Facebook!*

Contents

Introduction

In the days B.C. (Before Computers), losing touch with friends and family was a part of life. You'd graduate and all your school chums would wander off in different directions. You'd leave your job and lose valuable contacts. Aunts, uncles, and cousins would seem to fall off the face of the earth. Even keeping in touch with siblings hundreds or thousands of miles away was a challenge.

Facebook, with the help of computers and the Internet, has reversed that trend. Not only does it enable you to stay in touch with people, but it also facilitates the process of tracking down people you lost touch with years or decades ago. Facebook also provides numerous ways for you to engage and interact with all these folks daily—by sharing status updates, photos, and videos; posting links to favorite web pages or blogs; chatting; messaging (e-mailing); playing games; planning events; gathering in groups; and so on.

Perhaps best of all, Facebook is free, and all you need to get started is a computer with an Internet connection and a desire to connect with others. If you're concerned about privacy, you'll be relieved to know that Facebook gives you complete control over whom you choose to "friend" and the information you choose to share.

If you're concerned that you don't know where to start, that's where we come in. In this book, we provide everything you need to know to get started on Facebook; track down friends, family members, colleagues, former classmates, and others; and tap the full potential of Facebook.

Disclaimer: Facebook is in a constant state of change as its developers introduce new features and adjust the ways that Facebook members interact with the service and with one another. During the writing of the book we checked everything, step by step, not once, not twice, but three times to verify its accuracy prior to publication, but we're 99.99 percent sure that by the time you read this, something will have changed. We'll keep you up to date via our website at FacebookIdiot.com.

What You Learn in This Book

You don't have to read this book from cover to cover (although you might miss some succulent tidbits if you skip around). If you haven't even signed up with Facebook, start with Chapter 1 to register, log in, and take a brief tour of Facebook's core features. If you're concerned about privacy issues, skip to Chapter 6, where we show you how to adjust your privacy settings. To track down people and invite them to be your Facebook friends, head to Chapter 3. Chapter 7 shows you how to share photos, one of Facebook's most popular features.

As for the rest of the chapters, each covers a specific Facebook feature. To provide some structure for this hodgepodge of features, we've grouped the chapters into the following four parts and tacked on a glossary at the end:

Part 1, Mastering Facebook Basics, shows you how to sign up, sign in, add a photo and information to your Facebook Profile, track down friends and family and add them as Facebook friends, keep in touch with friends via Walls and News Feeds, contact people in private via the Message feature (a fancy name for e-mail), and tweak the privacy settings to your comfort level. We'll also show you how to leave Facebook with or without leaving personal information behind.

Part 2, Getting More Involved with Facebook, ramps you up to some more advanced Facebook features, including photo sharing, video sharing, groups, chat, events, and notes (sort of like blogging). After logging on and figuring out what the Wall and News Feed are all about, these are the features you tackle next.

Part 3, Harnessing the Power of Facebook Applications, introduces you to some higher-level applications (or apps for short) designed to enhance the Facebook experience. Here, you learn how to access core Facebook apps, explore Facebook's robust collection of third-party apps, use the Mobile app to access Facebook from your cell phone or other mobile communications device, and use the Marketplace app to shop for or sell stuff (or give stuff away, look for free stuff, find a job, or post a job opening).

Part 4, Getting Down to Business on Facebook, helps you unleash the power of social-media marketing on Facebook. After a brief chapter on how you can use Facebook to promote yourself, your business, or your products and services, we show you how to create and promote a business-based Facebook page (sometimes called a Fan page) and how to use Facebook ads to drive traffic to your website, blog, or page and strengthen your brand.

Conventions Used in This Book

We use several conventions in this book to make it easier to understand. For example, when you need to type something, it appears **bold.**

Likewise, if we tell you to select or click a command, the command also appears **bold.** This enables you to quickly scan a series of steps without having to wade through all the text.

Extras

A plethora of sidebars offer additional information about what you've just read. Here's what to look for:

FRIEND-LY ADVICE

During our days on Facebook, we've discovered easier, faster, and better ways to perform certain tasks and maximize the power of specific features. Here, we share these tips with you.

WHOA!

Before you click that button, skim the page for one of these boxes, each of which offers a precautionary note. Chances are, we've made the mistake ourselves, so let us tell you how to avoid the same blunder.

DEFINITION

Facebook uses its own distinct terminology to describe its features. For example, a Facebook friend may not actually be your friend in real life—he or she could be a relative or a co-worker or someone you just met on Facebook—but on Facebook, the person is your friend. Here, we crack the code.

NETIQUETTE

Every social venue has its rules of engagement—spoken or unspoken, written or unwritten. Break a rule, and you're likely to ruffle some feathers. To help you establish and maintain your good standing on Facebook, we use these boxes to call your attention to proper Facebook etiquette.

POKE

On Facebook, you can *poke* your Facebook friends when they're online to let them know you're thinking about them. As you might imagine, this can get annoying if someone overdoes it. We include pokes throughout the book to cue you in on lesser-known features of Facebook. Hopefully, you'll find our pokes more compelling than most.

Acknowledgments

Several people contributed to building and perfecting this book. We owe special thanks to Tom Stevens for choosing us to author this book and for handling the assorted details to get this book in gear. Thanks to Phil Kitchel and Jaime Julian Wagner for guiding the content of this book, keeping it focused on new users, ferreting out all our typos, and fine-tuning our sentences. Megan Douglass deserves a free trip to the Formula One race of her choosing for shepherding the manuscript (and art) through production. The Alpha Books production team merits a round of applause for transforming a collection of electronic files into such an attractive book.

We also owe special thanks to our publisher, Marie Butler-Knight, who personally reviewed the manuscript as she made her first foray into the world of Facebook. You can read her first-hand account of her initial encounters with Facebook by visiting FacebookIdiot.com and clicking the **From Marie** link under Categories.

Finally, we'd be remiss if we failed to thank the dozen or so Facebook members—our friends, both on and off Facebook—who allowed us to capture their Facebook activity in the screen shots you see throughout this book. To Adam Chase, Al Rotches, Andy Marker, Chris Ochs, Debra Oakland, Glenda Belicove, Jay Muntz, Jennifer Myers,

Michael McKenzie, PureFit Nutrition Bars, R. Scott Torgan, Stuart Lisonbee, and Susan Cherones, thank you very much; this book wouldn't have been possible without your witty status updates, photos, and more.

Trademarks

All terms mentioned in this book that are known to be or are suspected of being trademarks or service marks have been appropriately capitalized. Alpha Books and Penguin Group (USA) Inc. cannot attest to the accuracy of this information. Use of a term in this book should not be regarded as affecting the validity of any trademark or service mark.

Mastering Facebook Basics

Everyone on Facebook has had a first encounter with it—staring at the screen, bewildered as to what's going on, and uncertain on how to proceed. It's sort of like stepping foot in a foreign country, where you're uncertain of the customs and can't even figure out how to plug in your hair dryer without turning it into toast.

In this part, we re-create the first-encounter experience without the fear and bewilderment. We show you how to sign up, sign in, flesh out your profile, upload a Profile photo, protect your personal information, find people, make friends, and interact with others via Walls and News Feeds. In other words, we bring you up to speed on the basics.

Meeting Facebook Face to Face

In This Chapter

- Knowing what this Facebook thing is all about
- Getting your face on Facebook
- Making your way around
- Brushing up on Facebook etiquette
- Getting help

At your next party or family get-together, somebody is sure to mention Facebook. When they do, ask "What's Facebook?" The room is likely to fall silent (except for a few scattered giggles), and then everyone in the room who's had any experience with Facebook will start to trip over one another trying to explain it to you.

Everyone these days seems to be on Facebook … except you. Well, that's about to change. It's high time to lose your Facebook virginity and join the rest of your friends and family in the twenty-first century. In this chapter, we introduce you to Facebook, show you how to register and log in, and then take you on a nickel tour to get you up to speed on the basics.

What Is Facebook, Anyway?

Facebook is a free (so far, anyway), online, social-networking venue, where friends, family, colleagues, and acquaintances can mingle, get to know one another better, and expand their social circles.

After you register and log in to Facebook, as explained in the following section, you can invite people you know to join you on Facebook and become your *friend*. Any friends already on Facebook can invite you to become their Facebook friend, too. (We cover the whole making friends thing in Chapter 3.)

Once you have a Facebook friend or two, you can begin exchanging notes by posting *status updates* to your *News Feed*. A status update essentially tells your Facebook friends what you're doing, thinking, or feeling. Your News Feed is a running record of status updates and more posted by you and your friends. The "and more" can include photos and video clips that you and your friends post, links to interesting stuff on the web, notes you create, results of quizzes and polls you participate in, and more.

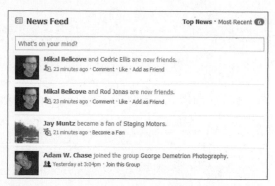

Your News Feed keeps you in touch with your friends.

That's Facebook in a nutshell, but you can do much more than simply swap text messages with your buddies. Following are some of the more popular activities you may want to engage in:

- Dig up old friends and classmates.

- Track down family members who've wandered from the fold.

- Expand your social and professional circles by connecting with friends of friends and current and former co-workers.

- Share photos, videos, and links to interesting web pages.

- Recommend books, movies, and music.

- Exchange birthday wishes and gifts.

- Play games.

- Spread the word about political causes and charities.

- Invite guests to parties and other get-togethers and keep track of who's planning to attend.

- Chat with your friends online ... assuming they're online when you are.

- Buy and sell stuff, find a job, and market yourself or your company.

POKE

Facebook is in a perpetual process of evolution. By the time you read this, additional features may be available. To keep up to date on new features, visit our website at FacebookIdiot.com.

Putting Your Face on Facebook

Before you can join the revelry, you have to put your face (and name) on Facebook by registering—entering your e-mail address, choosing a password, and providing some basic information about yourself, including your name, gender, and birthday:

1. Fire up your web browser and head to www.facebook.com.

2. Complete the Sign Up form. It will provide the instruction you need.

3. Click **Sign Up.** Facebook may display a security check screen prompting you to type a string of characters shown on the screen.

4. If a security check appears, type the text that appears as directed, click **Sign Up,** and proceed to the following section.

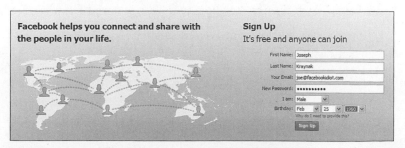

Complete the form and click **Sign Up.**

Finding Friends and Entering Your Info

After you register, Facebook steps you through the process of finding friends, entering basic information like schools you've attended
and places you've worked, and uploading a digital photo. All of these
steps are optional, so you can safely click **Skip** three times and do all
this later at your leisure. If you'd rather do it now, proceed to the following section.

Finding Friends Using Your E-Mail Address Book

The first order of business is to find some friends. If the e-mail
address you used to sign on to Facebook is web-based, like gmail
(Google e-mail), and your e-mail account has an address book with
contacts listed in it, Facebook can extract e-mail addresses from your
address book and use them to locate any Facebook members who log
in using any of those addresses.

Don't worry, Facebook won't send out friend invitations to everyone
in your address book without your permission. You'll have a chance
to select the people you want to invite. To find potential friends now,
enter the password associated with your e-mail account, click **Find
Friends,** and follow instructions. If you don't know your e-mail password, you will be unable to use this feature. Try contacting your
e-mail service provider to have your password reset. For more about
finding friends, see Chapter 3.

Facebook can find friends for you.

Entering School and Workplace Information

In Step 2 you're asked to enter information about your high school, college, and one place you've worked. Facebook will use this information to search for even more people you may know—people who graduated from the same high school or college the same year you did or who worked at the same company.

Enter any or all of the requested information and click **Save & Continue** or just click **Skip.**

Enter school and workplace information to enlist Facebook's assistance in tracking down classmates and co-workers.

If you choose **Save & Continue,** Facebook displays a selection of Facebook members it has identified as people with whom you may have graduated or worked. You can select any or all of these people and then click **Save & Continue** to invite them to be your friends. When you're done, Facebook displays the third step in getting started: uploading a photo of yourself, as discussed next.

Upload a Digital Photo of Yourself

If you have a digital photo of yourself stored on your computer, or a webcam plugged into your computer so you can take a photo of yourself, you can add your mug shot to your profile. In Step 3 of getting started, click **Upload a Photo** or **Take a Photo.**

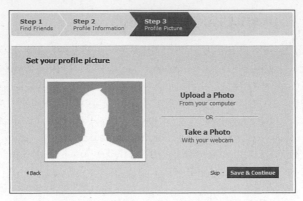

You can upload a photo or take a photo using a webcam.

If you click **Upload a Photo,** the Upload Your Profile Picture dialog box appears, prompting you to specify the photo file you want to use. Click **Browse,** use the resulting dialog box to select a digital photo of yourself stored on your computer, and click **Open.** Facebook uploads the photo and inserts it in your profile.

If you click **Take a Photo,** the Take a Photo dialog box appears. Click the **Camera** icon, say, "Cheese," into your webcam, and wait three seconds for Facebook to snap your photo. If you like what you see, click **Save Picture.** If you don't, click the **X** in the upper-right corner of the picture and reshoot.

You can snap a picture of yourself using a webcam.

Logging In and Logging Out

Now that you have a username (your e-mail address) and password, you can log in and out of Facebook whenever the spirit moves you. Just head to Facebook's Home page at www.facebook.com, type the e-mail address you used to register in the **E-mail** box, type your password in the **Password** box, and click **Login**. Facebook logs you in and displays your Home page, which features your News Feed and provides access to the rest of Facebook from one convenient location. To exit Facebook, click **Account, Logout** in the upper-right corner of the screen.

Enter your e-mail address and password to log on.

WHOA!

If someone else has access to your computer, log out when you're done on Facebook. Otherwise, someone can easily log in, read the discussions you're having with your friends, view your photos and videos, and post status updates pretending they're coming from you. They can even change your password!

In Your Face with the Interface

When you log in, Facebook gets in your face with all the buttons, bars, links, icons, and menus you need to access everything. Facebook has done a nice job of organizing all this stuff, but the interface can seem a little overwhelming at first. Here, we highlight the main areas you need to focus on, then describe them in more detail in the sections that follow.

Core features   Publisher   News Feed   Top menu

Games and bookmarked applications   Online chat

Facebook's interface.

Scooting Up to the Top Menu

The top menu (formerly known as "the blue bar") is Old Reliable. It appears at the top of the window no matter where you are or what you're doing on Facebook, providing quick access to the following features (from left to right on the bar):

- **Facebook:** Clicking the Facebook icon takes you Home—to the page that greets you when you sign on.

- **Friend Requests:** Click the **Friend Requests** icon, and a menu drops down displaying any Facebook members who are asking to be your friend. The menu also contains a Find Your Friends link you can click to search for your friends on Facebook. See Chapter 3 for more about friends.

- **Messages:** Click the **Messages** icon, and Facebook displays a list of any messages you received from other Facebook members. The menu also contains the Send a New Message link you can click to compose and send a message to someone on Facebook. See Chapter 5 for more about Facebook's Message (e-mail) feature.

- **Notifications:** Click the **Notifications** icon to view a list of your Facebook friends' current activities that pertain to you. Facebook notifies you whenever someone sends you a message, posts something on your wall, or comments on something you commented on.

- **Search:** Click in the **Search** box, type a search word or phrase, and press **Enter** or **Return** on your computer keyboard to search Facebook for people, places, things, or help with a particular feature.

- **Home:** Takes you to your Home page, where you can view your News Feed.

- **Profile:** Displays your Profile page, where you can access your Wall, information about yourself, your photo albums, and other items of interest. In Chapter 2, you learn how to edit your Profile. In Chapter 4, you meet the Wall.

- **Find Friends:** Takes you to the "We'd like to help you find your friends" page where you can search for people you know on Facebook and invite them to be your Facebook friends, so you can communicate with one another. You can also invite people you know who aren't Facebook members, but they'll have to join Facebook before you can become Facebook friends.

- **Account:** Click **Account,** and a menu drops down providing access to several options: Edit Friends, Account Settings, Privacy Settings, Application Settings, Help Center, and Logout. Edit Friends takes you to a screen where you can search for and add more Facebook friends. We'll provide more detail on the "Settings" options later in this chapter. The last two options are pretty obvious—you can get help or log out of Facebook.

Catching Up on Your News Feed

The News Feed is the core component of Facebook, providing you with a running account of just about everything you and your Facebook friends are up to and have agreed to share with one another. (In Chapter 6, you learn how to change your privacy settings if you want to share less than everything.)

You can switch your News Feed to display Top News or Most Recent by clicking the desired option just above the News Feed. Top News displays a list of what Facebook deems are the most interesting posts from your Facebook friends. Most Recent displays all your friends' posts, starting with the most recent.

Checking Out the Publisher

At the top of your News Feed is your own personal Publisher. Whenever you want to post something to your News Feed, click in the Publisher's text box (the box containing "What's on your mind?"), type your message, and click **Share.** In addition to text messages, you can post photos, videos, links, event announcements, notes, and other stuff you want to share. See Chapter 4 for a thorough explanation of the Publisher.

Exploring the Left Menu

The left menu (to the left of the News Feed) contains links for the most popular features on Facebook, such as:

- **You:** At the top of the left menu is your mug shot (assuming you added one), your name, and a link called View My Profile. Click any one of these, and Facebook displays your Profile page. See Chapter 2 for more about your Profile.

- **Core features:** The next section down provides links to gain quick access to the five core Facebook features: News Feed, Messages, Events, Photos, and Friends. More about all these features in later chapters.

- **Applications and Games:** This section contains links to Facebook's collections of applications and games, along with links to popular Facebook applications (apps for short), including ads, pages, and groups (discussion areas).

- **Chat with Friends:** Click the **Go Online** link (below Chat with Friends) to make yourself available to chat with any of your Facebook friends. This also opens the Chat menu (lower-right corner of the screen), displaying any of your friends who are online. You can click a friend's name to start chatting with them. See Chapter 10 for more about Facebook's Chat feature. To go offline, click the **Chat** option (lower-right corner of the screen), mouse over **Options,** and click **Go Offline.**

Exploring the Column on the Right

The column on the right contains a hodgepodge of items of varying importance, including lists of friend requests and suggestions, advertisements, highlights, events, and more links for finding friends.

Adjusting Your Account Settings

Facebook provides all sorts of ways to customize your experience, and it divides your options into three categories: account settings, privacy settings, and application settings. In Chapter 6, we tackle privacy issues and show you how to tweak your privacy settings to share more or less information in accordance with your personal preferences. In Chapter 13, you learn how to change your application settings. With those two out of the way, only account settings remain.

To change your account settings, click **Account** (in the top menu) and then **Account Settings.** Navigate the following tabs to enter your preferences:

- **Settings:** Most items on the Settings tab let you change information you entered when you registered with Facebook—your name, username, e-mail address, password, and security question. You can also link your account to other accounts, including Google, Yahoo!, and Myopenid, so when you log in to those accounts, you're automatically logged in to Facebook.

- **Networks:** On the Networks tab, you can join a network, change a region, and leave a network. For details on using networks to find friends, check out Chapter 3.

- **Notifications:** Whenever just about anything happens on Facebook that involves you, Facebook can send a notification to the e-mail address you used to register your account. You can use the options on the Notifications tab to enable or disable these e-mail notifications for certain actions and enable SMS (Short Message Service) options to be notified via your cell phone or other mobile device. (You can always see your notifications by logging on to Facebook and clicking the Notifications icon near the left end of the top menu.)

- **Mobile:** The Mobile tab provides options to enable or disable Facebook for use with your cell phone or other mobile device. Enabling the mobile features allows Facebook to send notifications to your mobile device and allows you to post status updates, search for phone numbers, and upload photos and videos from your phone. For more about using Facebook with your cell phone or mobile device, check out Chapter 15.

- **Language:** If Facebook displays its options in a language you don't understand, you can click the Language tab and select a different language.

- **Payments:** Don't panic! Facebook is free. However, if you engage in business transactions, such as buying gifts for your friends or purchasing online advertising, you can click the Payments tab to enter payment preferences (Visa, MasterCard, and so on) and choose your preferred currency (dollar, euro, yen, and so on) for displaying prices and credit card charges.

- **Facebook Ads:** If you're concerned about your name or photo showing up in an advertisement on Facebook, click the Facebook Ads tab to learn more about what Facebook allows and prohibits in terms of advertisers using member information. To prevent advertisers from using your name or photo in an ad, if Facebook allows this in the future, click the box next to **Allow ads on platform pages to show my information to** and click **No one.** If you don't want your social actions (such as becoming a fan of a company or product on Facebook) to appear in ads displayed to your confirmed friends, scroll down the page, open the list next to **Show my social actions in Facebook ads to** and click **No one.**

FRIEND-LY ADVICE

If you're tired of being notified every time one of your friends sneezes on Facebook, head to the Notifications settings to make some adjustments.

Following Facebook Rules and Etiquette

To flourish as a social-networking service, Facebook must provide enough freedom to allow members to express themselves, find one another, and exchange information, but not so much freedom that members are subject to harassment or having their personal infor mation published without their permission. As a result, Facebook has some rules for members to follow and etiquette guidelines to help members police their own behaviors.

Rules and Regulations

Facebook sets the rules that govern membership in its Terms of Service, which you can read in its entirety by scrolling down to the footer and clicking **Terms.** They basically boil down to the following do's and don'ts:

- Do provide accurate and current information in your profile.

- Don't use Facebook to do anything illegal, immoral, or unethical.

- Do respect the rights of other members.

- Don't spam.

- Don't collect user information for marketing purposes without Facebook's permission.

- Don't do anything malicious to Facebook, including uploading viruses or unleashing denial-of-service attacks.

Etiquette

In the world of social networking, the rules of etiquette carry about as much weight as the terms of service. They not only protect others from being exposed to ill-mannered behavior, but they also protect members from the embarrassment that often follows from failing to act in accordance with a community's social norms. Following are several etiquette guidelines every Facebook member should follow:

- Include a current, realistic, clean photo of yourself and only yourself in your profile.

- Proofread your profile and status updates before posting information.

- Respond to status updates regularly. You don't have to comment on every status update, but do express genuine interest in what's going on in your friends' lives.

- Don't friend just anybody. It cheapens your true friendships and could potentially expose your friends and what they say to people they'd rather not know. In addition, you may be judged by the company you keep and what that company shares on your Wall and in your News Feed.

- Don't over-poke. It gets annoying real fast. (Poking consists of pulling up a friend's profile, by clicking on her name or photo, and then clicking the Poke link below her photo. The recipient of the poke receives a message letting her know you've acknowledged her existence. It's kind of dopey, which is why you should do it rarely, if at all.)

- Ask for permission before tagging someone in a photo. More about tagging photos in Chapter 7.

- Watch your language. If you wouldn't say it front of your mom or your boss, don't say it on Facebook.

- Go easy on the selling. If you have something to sell, use the Facebook Marketplace (see Chapter 16). Remember, it's called social networking, not social selling.

Taking It Easy with Facebook Lite

If Facebook's platform, complete with all of its bells and whistles, feels overwhelming or too much for you to take in all at once, consider using Facebook Lite at lite.facebook.com.

Check out Facebook Lite for a more streamlined experience.

Recognizing the need for a simpler experience, especially for users who lack access to high-speed Internet connections, Facebook's developers launched Facebook Lite, a stripped-down version of the platform that allows you to create and view status updates, as well as post photos and videos, but not much else. Gone are many of the extras, such as applications and chat, that have made Facebook the all-in-one social-networking platform it is today.

Help! Navigating Facebook's Help System

Although we cover the most important stuff you need to know to use Facebook, we can't cover everything in such a limited space. If you need help with something that's not covered in this book, head to Facebook's Help system. Click **Account, Help Center.** Click an icon for the feature you need help with.

Facebook's Help Center has an icon for each of the most common features.

To search for a specific answer, click in the **Search** box near the top of the Help Center, type a search phrase that best expresses the question you have or the feature you need assistance with, and press **Enter.** Facebook displays a collection of links that most closely match your search. Click the link you think is most likely to provide the information you need.

To browse for help, click the feature you need help with and then follow the trail of links to the solution.

The Help System also includes a tab for Getting Started (in the left menu)—a great place for newbies to learn how to find friends, set up a profile, and navigate Facebook. The Safety tab offers guidance for protecting yourself and any teenagers you're responsible for on Facebook. For more about protecting yourself and your dependents from harm and keeping your information secure on Facebook, check out Chapter 6.

Quitting Facebook

For whatever reason, should you decide that you want out of Facebook, you have two exits: you can deactivate your account or delete it.

Deactivating Your Account

Deactivating your account leaves all your stuff intact. If you quit and get homesick for Facebook, you can always pick up where you left off. To deactivate your account, here's what you do:

1. Click **Account, Account Settings.**

2. In the lower-right corner of the Settings box, click **Deactivate.** Facebook displays the guilt screen, complete with photos of all the friends who will miss you very, very much. Don't look.

3. Scroll down the page to the deactivation options.

4. Click the reason that best describes why you're leaving Facebook.

5. (Optional) Click in the **Please explain further** box and type any additional explanation you'd like to pass along to the folks at Facebook. (Be nice, or at least respectful.)

6. (Optional) If you want to stop receiving e-mail notifications from Facebook whenever your friends invite you to do something or send you a message, click **Opt out of receiving future e-mails from Facebook.**

7. Click the **Deactivate My Account** button. Facebook deactivates your account and displays a message informing you how to return later if you change your mind.

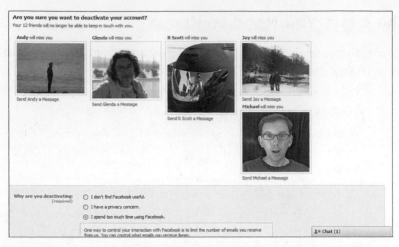

The guilt screen.

Deleting Your Account

Deleting an account is a more serious and long-term decision. Everything in your account is erased, including your photos, notes, list of friends, and so on. It's like getting rid of all your stuff and entering a witness-protection program.

If you're sure you want to delete your account, it's pretty simple. Head to https://ssl.facebook.com/help/contact.php?show_form= delete_account, click the **Submit** button, and respond to any confirmation warnings as desired. You're outta there.

*Want to quit? Click **Submit**.*

The Least You Need to Know

- To get on Facebook, go to www.facebook.com and then complete the sign up form and submit it.

- Your News Feed shows status updates, photos, videos, and other stuff you and your friends have chosen to share.

- To post something to your News Feed and Wall, click in the Publisher (top of the News Feed), type something, and click **Share.**

- To view your profile, click **Profile** (right end of the top menu).

- To return to the opening page, click the **Facebook** logo on the left end of the top menu or **Home** on the right end.

- You can get help at any time by clicking **Account** (upper-right corner of the screen) and then **Help Center.**

Fleshing Out Your Personal Profile

In This Chapter

- Building and editing your personal Profile
- Swapping out your Profile photograph
- Writing something clever about yourself
- Tweaking your personal and contact information

Without a personal Profile on Facebook, all you are is a name without a face, a skeleton, a nobody. Add a few details, including a photo, a brief bio, and some juicy personal and professional tidbits—and all of a sudden, you're somebody! In this chapter, we show you how to put some meat on those bones and hang a face on that name by filling out your Facebook Profile.

Accessing Your Profile to Adjust It

Before you can start tweaking your Profile, you have to get to it. In Facebook, three paths take you to the page where you can edit your Profile:

- Click **Profile** in the top menu at the top of any page.
- Click your name or **View My Profile** at the top of the column to the left of your News Feed.
- Click your photo or photo placeholder anywhere you see it in Facebook.

However you choose to get there, your Profile page appears. You can now mouse over your photo or photo placeholder to change your Profile photo, click the **Edit My Profile** link or the **Info** tab to edit information about yourself, or click the **Photos** tab to do more with photos.

Your Profile page looks something like this.

You can rearrange the Photos and Links boxes (but not your Information and Friends boxes) in the left sidebar. Rest the mouse pointer on the title bar of the box you want to move so that the pointer appears as a four-headed arrow. Then drag the box and drop it where you want it. Be prepared, however—moving a box isn't always as smooth as it should be.

WHOA!

Be careful what you include as part of your Profile. By default, friends and anyone in the networks you join (see Chapter 3) can view the information in your Profile, including your Birthday, Hometown, and Relationship Status. Your friends can view most of your contact information, too, including your phone number and address. You'll learn how to restrict access to this information in Chapter 6.

Changing Your Profile Photo

You can swap out your Profile photo at any time by uploading a new photo or snapping a photo with a webcam attached to your computer. As soon as you change photos, Facebook updates your photo in your Profile and wherever else it appears on Facebook, including your status updates—past, present, and future.

Prior to your photo shoot, review the following guidelines and suggestions for Profile photos:

- No porn—hard, soft, or otherwise.

- Use a current photo—making the wrinkles disappear by uploading an old high school photo is cheating.

- Use a photo of yourself—trying to pass yourself off as someone else is a violation of Facebook's terms of use.

- If someone else is in the photo, crop out that person. Otherwise, your friends may have to guess which one is you.

- Use a quality photo. If it's too dark, for example, use a photo-editing program to lighten it. Don't use a blurry photo—no amount of editing can fix a bad shot.

Uploading a Digital Photo

One of the best ways to add a Profile photo is to take a photo using a digital camera or scan in a photo of yourself. You can then adjust the brightness and contrast, if necessary; crop out any distractions in the background; save the image to your computer; and then upload it:

1. Click **Profile** in the top menu. Facebook displays your Profile page.

2. Mouse over your photo or photo placeholder. The Change Picture link appears.

3. Click **Change Picture.** A menu appears with several options for changing your Profile picture.

4. Click **Upload a Picture.** The Upload Your Profile Picture dialog box appears.

5. Click the **Browse** button. The Choose File to Upload dialog box appears.

6. Navigate to the disk drive and folder that contains the file you want to use.

7. Click the file's name.

8. Click **Open.** Facebook uploads the file (which can take a few seconds to a few minutes depending on the speed of your Internet connection) and then displays the Publish to Your Wall and Your Friends' Home pages? dialog box.

9. Either click **Skip,** which is what we usually do, or click in the **What's on your mind?** box, type a message about your photo to share with your friends, and click **Publish.** (We skip it, because our friends usually couldn't care less about us changing our Profile photos.) Either way, Facebook updates your Profile and uses the new photo for all of your comments and status updates.

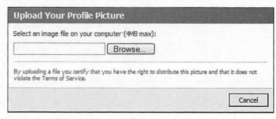

The Upload Your Profile Picture dialog box prompts you to select a picture file.

Snapping a Photo with Your Webcam

If you have a functioning webcam, you can take a photo of yourself sitting at your computer and have Facebook upload it to your Profile.

FRIEND-LY ADVICE

When snapping your own mug shot, look directly into the webcam instead of at your computer screen—that way, when your friends look at your Profile, you won't appear as though you're staring at their midsection or over the top of their head.

To snap a photo with your webcam, here's what you do:

1. Click **Profile** in the top menu. Facebook displays your Profile page.

2. Mouse over your photo. The Change Picture link appears.

3. Click **Change Picture.** A menu appears with several options for changing your Profile picture.

4. Click **Take a Picture.** The Take a Profile Picture dialog box appears.

5. Click the **Camera** icon and strike a pose. Facebook counts down three seconds and snaps your photo.

6. Preview your photo, and then do one of the following:

   If you don't like what you see, click the **X** in the upper-right corner of the picture and go back to Step 5 to reshoot.

   If the photo is acceptable, click **Save Picture.** Facebook uploads the file, which can take a few seconds to a few minutes, and then displays the Publish to Your Wall and Your Friends' Home pages? dialog box.

7. Either click **Skip,** which is what we usually do, or click in the **What's on your mind?** box, type a message about your photo to share with your friends, and click **Publish.** (We skip it, because our friends usually couldn't care less about us changing our Profile photos.) Either way, Facebook updates your Profile and uses the new photo for all of your comments and status updates.

The Take a Profile Picture dialog box prompts you to snap a photo of yourself by clicking the camera icon.

Selecting a Picture for Your Profile

As you upload Profile photos from your computer and shoot Profile photos using a webcam, Facebook places them in your Profile Pictures album. You can then select which Profile photo you want to use.

To choose a different photo from your collection, click **Profile** in the top menu, mouse over your photo, and click **Change Picture.** Click **Choose from Album,** click the photo you want to use, and click **Make Profile Picture.** Facebook displays the photo you just selected in your Profile and status updates.

You can delete a Profile photo by performing these same steps and clicking **Delete Photo.** When Facebook prompts you to confirm, click **Delete.** For more about managing your photos, check out Chapter 7.

You can make the selected photo your Profile picture.

Clipping Your Thumbnail

When you post a Profile photo, Facebook fits it inside the little box allocated for your mug shot. You don't have any control over how much of your photo is visible, but you do have a little control over how it fits in the box.

Click **Profile,** mouse over your photo, click **Change Picture,** and click **Edit Thumbnail.** In the Edit Thumbnail dialog box, hold the mouse over the picture until the four-headed arrow appears, then drag the thumbnail up, down, left, or right to change its position in the box. When it looks just right, click **Save.**

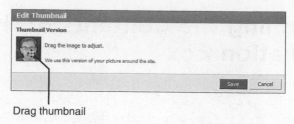

Drag thumbnail

Drag your photo in the preview box.

Adding a Blurb About Yourself

You can include a brief message below your photo on your Profile page. Your message may consist of a brief bio, a witty quote, your mission statement, or anything you like. Most folks who choose to include something generally keep their messages very brief.

To add a message, click **Write something about yourself,** and start typing. When you're done, click a blank area outside the box to save your changes and post them to your Profile. Now instead of "Write something about yourself" you see what you wrote about yourself.

Type your blurb

Write something about yourself.

FRIEND-LY ADVICE

You can always edit what you typed about yourself. Click the **Edit** icon in the upper-right corner of the box. (The Edit icon looks like a pencil.) Edit the message and then click a blank area outside the box to save your changes.

Controlling the Contents of the Information Box

A hop and a skip down from your Profile photo is an Information box that displays a couple tidbits about you—perhaps your relationship status and birthday. You can control what appears inside this box to limit what your friends and people in your network see when they visit your Profile.

Click the **Edit** icon in the upper-right corner of the Information box. A menu appears displaying checkboxes for all the items you can display in the box. Click the empty box next to each item you want to add to the display. Click the checked box next to each item appearing in the box that you want to exclude. As you check and uncheck items, Facebook automatically updates the display.

You choose what appears in your Information box.

Editing Information About Yourself

When you registered with Facebook, you entered a little information about yourself to get started. You can edit and add to this information any time to flesh out your Profile. To edit your Profile, do one of the following.

- Click **Profile** and then click **Edit My Profile** (below your Profile photo).

- Click **Profile** and then click the **Info** tab and click **Edit information** above and to the right of your Basic Information.

This takes you to a page with four sections: Basic Information, Personal Information, Contact Information, and Education and Work. To expand a section of the form, so you can edit its information, click the gray bar for that section. You can then edit your information, as described in the following sections.

Basic Information

Basic information goes slightly beyond name, rank, and serial number. It includes your Sex (and whether to display it in your Profile), Birthday, Hometown (and Neighborhood), Family Members, Relationship Status, Political Views, Religious Views, and several other items of interest. Simply complete the form as you would fill out any online form.

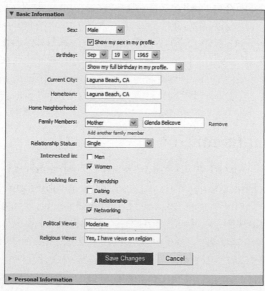

You can edit, add, or remove basic information about yourself.

Most of the items are pretty straightforward, except for Family Members and Relationship Status. To specify a family relationship, open the **Select Relation:** list and click the relation you are to the person you want to add as a family member; for example, Father, Mother, Sister, or Brother. Then click in the box to the right of your selection and type the person's name. As you type, a list of Facebook members whose names match what you've typed will appear, and you can click a member from the list. If you don't see a match, Facebook will prompt you for the person's e-mail address (after you choose to save your changes) so it can send the person an invitation to join Facebook.

 POKE

You add a family member only by entering the name of the person you want to add. You can't just say you have a son or daughter, for example, without supplying the name of your son or daughter.

For Relationship Status, you have several choices, including Married, Single, Engaged, and It's Complicated. You don't need to specify the individual you're having a relationship with, but you do have that option. If you'd like to specify the name of your significant other, click the box below your Relationship Status and start typing the appropriate name. As you type, a list of your Facebook friends whose names match what you've typed will appear, and you can click a member from the list. If you don't see a match, Facebook will prompt you for the person's e-mail address (after you choose to save your changes) so it can send the person an invitation to join Facebook.

Personal Information

When you're ready to get personal with your friends, you'll want to share more details about yourself, including hobbies and interests; favorite books, music, movies, and television shows; quotations you like; and perhaps even a brief bio. You can share any or all of this information by clicking the **Personal Information** bar, typing your information in each box, and clicking the **Save** button.

▼ Personal Information

Activities:	Running, Photography, Playing Tennis, Travel
Interests:	Social Media, Friends, Family
Favorite Music:	Just Say Yes by Snow Patrol Kisses and Cake by John Powell I'd Rather Be with You by Joshua Radin The Bridge to the Island by Jason Feddy This Life by Marc Ribbler
Favorite TV Shows:	Brotherhood Fringe Seinfeld Everybody Loves Raymond Two-and-a-half Men
Favorite Movies:	Hot Fuzz The Affair of the Necklace Italian Job Oceans 11-13 The Thomas Crown Affair
Favorite Books:	Into The Wild

You can get personal by sharing more about yourself.

Contact Information

If you want your friends to be able to get in touch with you out-side the confines of Facebook, include your contact information. Facebook already has the e-mail address you used to register, but you can add phone numbers, your mailing address, your website address, and even IM (Instant Messaging) screen names. Just click the **Contact Information** bar and supply as much or as little contact information as you like.

WHOA!

Share with care. We recommend omitting your home address and phone numbers. If a friend wants to call or visit, they can e-mail you to request that information. Sure, given your full name and hometown, just about anyone can track you down, but you don't have to make it easy for *just anyone* to show up on your doorstep or call you on your phone. For addi-tional details on protecting your privacy, check out Chapter 6.

Education and Work

When you signed up for Facebook, it asked for information about schools you attended and places you worked. Facebook can then use this information to help you track down friends and help classmates and co-workers find you.

If you skipped that part, or would like to edit or add entries, you can do so at any time. Just head to your Profile, click the link to edit it, click the gray **Education and Work** bar, and enter your changes.

In the Education and Work section, you can also add or remove schools or jobs. If you listed any colleges you attended, the form includes text boxes for entering up to three majors or areas of concentration, but you can add more, if you'd like.

The Least You Need to Know

- To edit your Profile, click **Profile** (in the top menu at the top of any page) and then click **Edit My Profile** (below your photo or the photo placeholder).

- After you choose to edit your Profile, click the bar for the section you want to edit: Basic Information, Personal Information, Contact Information, or Education and Work.

- Carefully choose which information you share, but include enough for family, friends, and co-workers to find and friend you.

- Upload or change your Profile image by mousing over your photo or photo placeholder and clicking **Change Picture.**

Connecting with Friends, Family, and Classmates

In This Chapter

- Sharing with Facebook friends
- Scouring Facebook and beyond for people you know
- Making and managing friends
- Exposing yourself to more potential friends

In real life, you're not just you. You are the sum total of yourself, your past, your aspirations, and everyone with whom you interact—friends, family members, colleagues, and even those strangers you're about to meet.

The same is true on Facebook, only more so. When you first register and log in, all you are is a name. When you start to connect with friends, family members, colleagues, and former classmates—and they start connecting with you—you become part of a thriving community. Each new Facebook friend adds a stitch to the tapestry that's you. In short, to get anything *out of* Facebook, you need to get *into* Facebook and get connected. This chapter shows you how.

Knowing What It Means to Be a Friend

On Facebook, your friends have benefits that others on Facebook may not have, depending on your privacy settings (see Chapter 6). They can read your Profile, for example, and follow discussions among you and your other friends. When you "friend" someone on Facebook, you give them access to information about yourself and your friends that could be sensitive or confidential, so you'd better have a pretty clear idea of who your friends are and what you're sharing with them before you start adding people to your inner circle.

> **WHOA!**
>
> You have complete control over what appears on your Facebook Wall and what's shared among friends, as we'll cover in Chapter 6. Until you learn those tricks, choose your friends and what you share very carefully and assume everything you post is publicly accessible. If you receive a friend request from someone you don't know, ignore it for now.

Sharing Walls and News Feeds

Friends share *News Feeds* and *Walls*, which may seem a little odd right now, but you'll get the idea in Chapter 4. For now, just keep in mind that whatever you post in your News Feed shows up on your friends' News Feeds and vice versa. In other words, if you add your mom as a friend, she'll be able to see whatever you post in your News Feed. Post a message about the wild time you had at that party Friday night, and Mom can see it.

Your Wall, on the other hand, is a quieter place, displaying only your posts and anything your friends have specifically posted to your Wall. However, whatever you or your friends post on your Wall or you post on theirs may show up in your News Feed and theirs. In Chapter 4, you learn more about the Wall and News Feed.

Sharing Photo Albums

When you upload photos to your account, your friends have access to those photos. You can restrict access to photos, as we'll explain in Chapter 7, but until you learn how to do that, hold off on posting anything too risqué or revealing. Even if your photos are accessible only to your friends, they might decide to share those photos with others—some of whom you might not want looking at those photos.

Friends can also "tag" you in a photo that they or someone they know has uploaded to Facebook. Tagging means that the photo is labeled with your name and will link to your Profile, which is kind of cool until someone tags you in an embarrassing pose (or embarrassing clothes—oh, those '80s!) and that tag is broadcast to all your friends, family, and co-workers. In Chapter 6, we show you how to keep those tag notifications to yourself. In Chapter 7, you learn how to add and remove tags.

Sharing Information

Unless you indicate otherwise, most of your Profile information is readily accessible to all your Facebook friends. This includes Basic Information, Personal Information, Contact Information (address, phone number, but not your e-mail address, unless you choose to share it), Education and Work experience, and a list of any groups you've joined. (See Chapter 9 for more about the Groups feature.)

In Chapter 6, you learn how to hide sensitive information from prying eyes. Until then, become friends only with people you don't mind having access to your information.

Digging Up People You Know

The whole purpose of Facebook is to facilitate connections among people, and since you have to find people before you can connect with them, Facebook features several ways to locate the people you know ... assuming, of course, they're on Facebook.

What about all those folks you know who aren't on Facebook yet? No worries—Facebook provides a way to invite them to join!

After you make a few friends, Facebook may display friends of theirs and suggest you invite them to be your friends. All you need to do is click the person's name in the Suggestions box or the "We'd like to help you find your friends" page, and follow the on-screen cues to send a friend request. More information on sending a friend request is provided later in this chapter.

Searching for an Individual by Name or E-Mail

One of the easiest ways to dig up a specific individual on Facebook is to perform a search:

1. Click **Friends** (in the left menu) or click **Find Friends** (in the top menu). The Find people you know on Facebook page appears.

2. Scroll down to the **Search for People** section.

3. Click in the **Search for People** box and type the name of the person you're looking for. You can type just the last name or a partial name to broaden your search.

4. Click the **Search** button, just to the right of what you typed (the Search button looks like a magnifying glass). Facebook performs the search, and if it finds any matches, it displays them as shown in the following figure.

5. Click the person's name or photo for more information about them. Unless you're already friends with this person, you'll probably see very little information. To invite the person to become your friend, skip ahead to the section on befriending and de-friending in this chapter.

6. If the search returns too many matches, you can filter the search results by typing entries in the **Location, School,** and/or **Workplace** boxes above the search results and then clicking the **Refine Search** button.

Searching for a specific name on Facebook turns up a list of matches.

FRIEND-LY ADVICE

If you know the person's e-mail address, try searching for that instead of the person's name. An e-mail address is more likely to turn up the individual you're looking for and screen out all the others.

Searching for People in Your Imported E-Mail Address Book

Facebook can use your e-mail address book to track down people you already keep in touch with. You can import addresses from a web-based e-mail account, such as Google Mail or Yahoo! Mail, or directly from Microsoft Outlook. If you use some other e-mail program or do not want to give Facebook access to your web-based e-mail account for any reason, you can export the address book from your e-mail program, save it as a file to your computer, and then import the addresses into Facebook.

Following are the steps for importing addresses from a web-based e-mail program. After these steps, we cover a couple variations you'll run into if you're using a different type of e-mail program or would rather not give Facebook access to your web-based account.

1. Click **Friends** in the left menu or **Find Friends** in the top menu. The We'd like to help you find your friends page appears.

2. Under Find People You Email, enter the e-mail address and password you use to log in to your web-based e-mail program and click **Find Friends.** Facebook displays a list of any Facebook members who've registered using any of the e-mail addresses in your address book.

3. Click the contacts you want to add as friends. (You can deselect contacts by clicking them again.)

4. Select any of your contacts not on Facebook that you want to invite. Facebook will invite nonmembers to become members so they can be your Facebook friends.

5. Click **Add as Friends.** Facebook will e-mail your friend request to everyone you selected.

Facebook can log in to your web-based e-mail program and import your e-mail addresses.

FRIEND-LY ADVICE

In addition to finding people you e-mail, Facebook can help you find people you IM (instant message) using AOL Instant Messenger, ICQ Chat, or Windows Live Messenger. Just head to the We'd like to help you find your friends page, scroll down to the Find People You IM section, click the link for the instant messaging program you use, and follow the instructions.

If you use Outlook to manage your e-mail (not Outlook Express, but the full version of Outlook that comes with Microsoft Office), click **Upload Contact File,** make sure **Automatically import my contacts from Outlook** is selected, and click **Find Friends.** Facebook scours Outlook and displays a list of Facebook members who've registered with any of the addresses. Select the contacts you want to add as friends, click **Add as Friends,** and follow the on-screen instructions to complete the operation.

Facebook prompts you to select people to invite as friends.

If you use some other e-mail client on your computer, such as Outlook Express or Mozilla Thunderbird, click **Upload Contact File,** click **Upload a contact file,** and then click **How to create a contact file ….** This displays a list of links you can click for instructions on how to export an address book from any of several popular e-mail programs. Click the link for your e-mail program and follow the instructions to export your address book.

After exporting your address book to a file on your computer, head back to the We'd like to help you find your friends page. Click **Browse,** use the resulting dialog box to select the e-mail address file you want to import, click **Open,** and then click **Find Friends.** Select the name of each person you want to invite to be your friend, and click **Add as Friends.**

Finding Old Classmates

When you completed your Profile, as shown in Chapter 2, you may have specified schools from which you graduated and your year of graduation. Assuming some of your classmates entered the same school and graduation year into their Profiles, you can have Facebook track them down for you.

Click **Friends** in the left menu or **Find Friends** in the top menu. Scroll down near the bottom of the screen (under the Search for People box), and click the **Find classmates** link for the school you attended. Facebook presents you with a list of people, many of whom should be your fellow alumni.

Connecting with Co-Workers

When you're ready to socialize or network with current or former co-workers, Facebook can help. Click **Friends** in the left menu or **Find Friends** in the top menu. Scroll down near the bottom of the screen (under the Search for People box), and click the **Find coworkers** link for one of the companies where you work or worked. Facebook presents you with a list of people who reported working at the same company.

If you didn't add one of the companies you worked for or one of the schools you attended to your Profile, you can still search for classmates or co-workers. After performing a search for classmates or co-workers, scroll to the bottom of the list, where you'll find a form for searching by company or school. You can type any company or school name into this form.

WHOA!

Think twice about friending colleagues and co-workers. We've heard plenty of stories about co-workers passing along embarrassing and sometimes career-ending status updates that were read by other co-workers and even the boss. If you do friend a colleague, be especially careful about anything you post about your job, office politics, or other colleagues.

Befriending and De-Friending

Becoming friends on Facebook requires mutual agreement. One member initiates the process by sending a friend request. The other member must then accept the invitation to confirm the arrangement.

In the following sections, you discover how to send and respond to friend requests, de-friend someone with whom you no longer wish to associate, and group your friends using friend lists to help you navigate your various social circles.

Sending a Friend Request

You can bump into prospective friends all sorts of ways on Facebook. Someone can send you a friend request, you can track down the person by performing a search, your current friends can offer suggestions, or Facebook may display a list of suggested friends.

However you happen to bump into a person, the process for inviting them to become your friend is always the same: click **Add as Friend** and use the resulting dialog box to send your request. You can click **Send Request** or click **Add a personal message** and type a greeting before clicking **Send Request.**

Your friend must confirm your request before Facebook establishes a connection.

Send a friend request to initiate a new friendship.

Responding to a Friend Request

When someone sends you a friend request, you typically receive an e-mail message with a link you can click to go to Facebook and respond to the request. If you don't check your e-mail very often or have chosen not to receive e-mail notifications, you can check for incoming friend requests by logging on to Facebook and checking the Requests list at the top of the right column.

Click the **friend request** link to view the requests. Every friend request includes the person's name and the number of friends you have in common, if any. You can click the person's name to check out her Profile or click the **Mutual Friends** link to find out which friends you have in common.

After accessing the friend requests list, you can click one of the following options for any individual on the list.

- **Confirm,** to accept the invitation and become friends.

- **Ignore,** to snub the person and delete the request. Don't worry, Facebook is polite. It doesn't send a message like "Your recent friend request has been REJECTED, LOSER!" It just doesn't send anything.

- **Send Message,** to e-mail the person without confirming or ignoring the request. You may want to send the person a message, for example, asking how you two know each other.

You can confirm or ignore a friend request.

Dumping a Friend

If you've added a friend by mistake, or decide later that you really don't want the person hanging out in your Face-space, you can de-friend the person. Here's what you do:

1. Click **Profile** (in the top menu).

2. Under Friends (in the left menu), click **See All.**

3. Click the **X** next to the person's name. The Remove Connection dialog box appears, prompting you to confirm.

4. Click **Remove** to de-friend the person or **Cancel** to give them another chance.

NETIQUETTE

Even though Facebook doesn't notify your friend of your decision to de-friend, it can result in an awkward situation if your former friend tries to post something to your Wall and can't get to it. If you decide to re-friend, you have to go through the whole friend-request thing again, which could raise some questions.

Creating and Managing Friend Lists

If you're like most people, you have multiple social circles—family members, grade school classmates, high school classmates, co-workers and colleagues, and perhaps even members of your reading club. Unfortunately, your News Feed shows a mish-mash of all your friends' posts and updates, making the task of sorting out communications within each social circle nearly impossible.

Facebook's Friend List feature can make your social circles more manageable by assigning your friends to individual lists. After creating a friend list, you can use it to do the following:

- When viewing your News Feed (see Chapter 4), click a friend list to hide posts from everyone except the friends on the selected list.

- Send an e-mail message to everyone on the friend list without having to address it to each and every individual. (See Chapter 5 for more about Facebook's Messages feature—an internal e-mail feature.)

- Send an event announcement and invitation to everyone on the friend list without having to address it to each and every individual. (See Chapter 11.)

- Tighten or loosen restrictions on your Profile for different friend lists. (See Chapter 6 for more about Facebook privacy settings.)

Consider starting with some basic lists, such as having a separate list for each of the following circles: family members, friends, and co-workers.

WHOA!

A friend list merely filters what appears in your News Feed. Don't make the common mistake of believing that you can post status updates to one friend list without your other friends seeing it. All of your friends are privy to whatever you post, unless you edit the Custom Privacy setting for the status update in question. See Chapter 4 for details about changing privacy settings for individual posts.

To create a friend list and assign some friends to it, here's what you do:

1. Click **Account** (in the top menu), then click **Edit Friends** from the drop down menu.

2. In the left menu, below any existing lists (under **Lists**), click **+ Create.** The Create New List dialog box appears.

3. Click in the **Enter a name** box and type a name for the list, such as Co-workers, Family, or People I Used to Date.

4. Scroll through the names and images and click each friend you want to include in this list. (If you click a friend by mistake, click the friend again to deselect her.) If your friend list is really long and difficult to scroll through, you can type each friend's name and select each friend that way instead.

5. Click **Create List.** Facebook creates the list and displays it in the left menu, under Lists.

You can create a friend list and assign friends to it.

You can edit a friend list at any time. Click **Account, Edit Friends.** Under Lists (left menu) click the friend list you want to edit, and then click the **Edit List** button (above the list). This displays a dialog box in which you can change the name of the list and add or remove people from it.

To delete a friend list, click **Account, Edit Friends.** Under Lists (left menu), click the friend list you want to delete and then click the **Delete List** button above the list. Facebook displays a dialog box warning that deleting the list is not reversible and asking for your confirmation. Click **Delete List** to confirm or **Cancel** to abort the operation.

 POKE

> While deleting a list is irreversible, it doesn't permanently remove your friends from your complete list of friends, so you can always re-create the list—assuming you remember who was on it.

Expanding Your Reach with Networks

When you signed up for Facebook, the registration routine asked for information about where you live, the schools you've attended, and even about the places you've worked. It uses this information to help find people you might know and want to connect with via Facebook. If you'd like to make your Profile (and perhaps other content, such as photos) available to more people, consider joining one or more networks, each of which is based around a workplace, region, high school, or college.

With the Network feature, you can relax restrictions on your Profile for people in a network, so they can see more about you than people outside the network can see. To join a network, here's what you do:

1. Click **Account** (in the top menu) and click **Account Settings.** The Account Settings page appears.

2. Click the **Networks** tab.

3. Click in the **Network name** box and start typing the name of your workplace, city, state, high school, or college. As you type, Facebook displays networks that match what you've typed so far.

4. Click the name of the network you want to join. In some cases, the network may require additional information, including a valid e-mail address provided by the school, company, or organization.

5. Enter any information you're prompted to supply.

6. Click **Join Network.** Facebook updates the Networks page showing that you're now an active member of the network you just joined.

> **POKE**
>
> If you can't find a Network you think Facebook should have, Facebook might be willing to add the Network for you. Visit www.facebook.com/ help/?faq=13287 for more information on how to contact Facebook about adding a new Network.

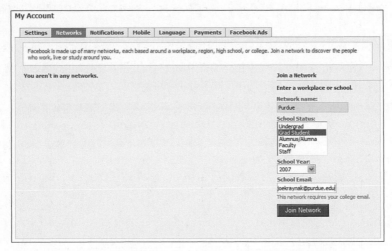

You can join networks to gain exposure to more potential friends.

You can leave a network at any time. Click **Settings, Account Settings,** and the **Networks** tab, and then click **Leave Network** next to the network you want to leave.

The Least You Need to Know

- Be selective when friending people on Facebook. Friends can view and access each other's status updates, Walls, and other content.

- To search for someone on Facebook, click **Friends** (in the left menu) or **Find Friends** (in the top menu), scroll down and click in the **Search for People** box, type the name or partial name of the person, and press **Enter.**

- When you receive a friend request, you have three options: Confirm, Ignore, or Send Message.

- Use friend lists to group friends and reduce some of the clutter in your News Feed.

- To dump a friend, click **Profile** (in the top menu), click **See All** (in the left menu under Friends), and click **X** next to the name of the person you want to de-friend.

Hitting the Wall ...
and Your News
Feed

In This Chapter

- Understanding the difference between your Wall and News Feed
- Configuring your Wall and filtering its content
- Creating and posting status updates of your own
- Commenting on friends' status updates
- Posting messages on friends' Walls
- Sharing your friends' content with other friends

Facebook provides two major modes of communication between and among friends—the *Wall* and *News Feed*. Your News Feed greets you whenever you log on. It's the column in the middle of the screen that asks, "What's on your mind?" and displays recent status updates your friends have posted, along with other information—such as when a friend edits his Profile or takes a quiz. If you wander away from your News Feed, you can always return to it by clicking **Home** or **Facebook** in the blue navigation bar at the top of any page.

Your Wall, on the other hand, is a more intimate place that displays only your posts, anything your friends have specifically posted to your Wall, and any Wall-to-Wall discussions you're having with your friends. You can view your Wall at any time by clicking **Profile** (in the top menu) or clicking your name or photo in the left menu.

When you click a friend's name, you're taken to that friend's Profile page, where you can read his Wall posts and post messages to this particular friend. As you reply to one another's Wall posts, you engage in a Wall-to-Wall discussion that appears on both your Walls.

WHOA!

Communicating via Walls reduces the frenetic clutter of status updates characteristic of the News Feed, but Wall-to-Wall discussions are not private. Anyone who can access your Wall or your friend's Wall can read the content of your posts, and some Wall posts may show up in your mutual friends' News Feeds. You can restrict access to your Wall by adjusting your privacy settings, as discussed in Chapter 6.

In the following sections, you get a better feel for your News Feed and Wall, as you navigate, post status updates, and customize these two areas.

Homing In on Your News Feed

You can't miss your News Feed. Log on to Facebook, and it's right there, in your face, front and center. To filter out some of the "noise" and focus on the most important news of the day, Facebook's default setting for the News Feed is Top News. Facebook hides most of the status updates, displaying only the most important ones. To deem what's most important, Facebook considers numerous factors, including the number of friends commenting on a certain post, which friends posted the items, and the type of content (photo, video, status update, or link).

To view every single status update from every one of your friends, which can get pretty cluttered and difficult to follow, click **Most Recent** (above your News Feed and off to the right).

However, as soon as you gather enough friends, assuming they're fairly active on Facebook, that News Feed can become very cluttered. The information you really want to see can easily get buried in a barrage of status updates, photos, videos, links, and events.

Fortunately, you can select the type of content you want to view by clicking the desired option in the left menu. Click any of the following options to reduce the clutter:

- **Welcome:** This option displays a page offering to step you through the process of getting started on Facebook. If this seems like deja vu all over again, it is, but if you feel like you missed something the first time around, you can get a fresh start here.

- **News Feed:** This is your ticket back to the News Feed, just in case you wandered off and want to return.

- **Messages:** Click **Messages** to check your inbox for any messages your friends or other Facebook members have sent you. See Chapter 5 for details.

- **Events:** If you registered for any events or scheduled events of your own, you can click **Events** to display a list of events along with any recent news or updates relating to them.

- **Photos:** Display only photos posted by you and your friends. For more about photos, check out Chapter 7. When you click Photos, a submenu appears that provides access to Video (posted by you and your friends), Recent Albums (the most recent photos your friends have posted), Mobile Uploads (photos and videos your friends have taken using a mobile device and uploaded to Facebook), and My Uploads (photos and videos you've shot using a mobile device and uploaded to Facebook).

- **Friends:** Clicking Friends displays a page that enables you to manage your Facebook friends. At the very top of the page are any friend requests you've received and haven't yet responded to. The rest of the page contains several sections devoted to helping you find friends. When you click Friends, a submenu appears with two options—Status Updates and Recently Updated—followed by any friend lists you created (see Chapter 3). Click **Recently Updated** to display outstanding friend requests plus a list of any updates your friends have made to their profiles. Click **Status Updates** to view a streamlined News Feed displaying only the text portions of your and your friends' status updates, along with any comments posted to those updates—no photos, videos, links, or events. Click a friend list to view status updates posted only by friends included in that list.

Click Most Recent to view all status updates as they're posted ⌐
Click Top News to focus on the most important updates ⌐

You can view all posts listed from newest to oldest or focus on the Top News.

You can always return to displaying a complete list of status updates by clicking **News Feed** near the top of the left navigation bar.

Checking Out Your Wall

If "good fences make good neighbors," Walls on Facebook make the best of friends. On Facebook, Walls aren't used to wall in or wall out. They're used to communicate, sort of like a graffiti artist uses walls as his canvas to broadcast messages.

In the following sections, you find out how to access your Wall and your friends' Walls, configure your Wall, and use Walls to carry on more direct conversations with a friend.

Heading to Your Wall

Your Wall is your own space on Facebook. It's what your friends see when they click your name or photo. It's also what you see when you click your name or photo or click **Profile** in the top menu.

Your Wall displays your status updates and content that friends have posted to your Wall.

Configuring Your Wall

You can't exactly configure your Wall with a colorful background and fancy fonts, but you can configure it in terms of the information it displays. First, click **Options** (just above your Wall posts) to access the following choices:

- **You + Friends:** This is the default setting. You see everything you and your friends have posted on your Wall.

- **Just You:** Displays only your activity.

- **Just Friends:** Displays only your friends' posts to your Wall.

- **Settings:** Offers additional configuration options, including Stories Posted by You (on sites outside Facebook), Profile Story Comments (whether you want comments for each update included in the display by default), Stories Posted by friends (to control who can post on your Wall and who can see what others have posted on your Wall), and Application Settings (to control which applications can post on your Wall).

Filter the content on your Wall

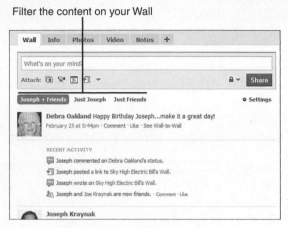

You can filter your Wall's content.

Bumping Into a Friend's Wall

Except for the content posted on it, a friend's Wall looks almost identical to your own Wall and contains many of the same features, though they may be called something different. For example, under your friend's Status Update box, instead of Options, you see Filters. Click **Filters,** and you can display status updates for Your Friend + Friends, Just Your Friend, Just Friends, or Wall-to-Wall (discussions exclusively between you and this particular friend).

Filter the content on your friend's Wall

You can filter the content displayed on your friend's Wall.

Posting to Your Wall or News Feed

At the top of the News Feed and the Wall is Facebook's Publisher. Its primary purpose is to enable you to post text informing your friends of what you're doing, planning to do, thinking, or feeling at this very moment. It's very similar to posting a "tweet" on Twitter.com—something referred to as microblogging. You use the Publisher to post status updates (also called stories) and other content to your News Feed or Wall or to a friend's Wall.

Adding a post to your News Feed or Wall is one of the easiest things you can possibly do on Facebook:

1. Click **Home** or **Profile** (in the top menu) to post in your News Feed or on your Wall. Either way, what you post will appear in both your News Feed and on your Wall. (Click a friend to post the update to your friend's Wall, addressing the post more directly to this particular friend.)

2. Click in the **What's on your mind?** box and type your message.

3. (Optional) Click any of the controls below the What's on your mind? box to add a photo, video, link, event announcement, or other content to your status update, as explained in the following sections.

4. (Optional) Click the privacy button (the button with the lock on it below and toward the right of where you typed your message) and click the desired privacy option:

- **Everyone:** All Facebook members can read your post.

- **Friends of Friends:** Only your Facebook friends and their friends can read your post.

- **Only Friends:** Only your Facebook friends can read the post. (This is the default setting.)

- **Customize:** Displays the Custom Privacy dialog box that provides additional control over who can read your post. If you have one or more friend lists, this comes in very handy for sharing a post with a select group of friends.

5. Click **Share.** Facebook displays the update in the News Feed or on the Wall where you posted it.

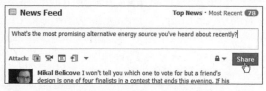

Post a status update to keep your friends informed about what you're up to.

Attaching a Photo

Most people love viewing photos, particularly interesting photos of people they know and love, so consider including an occasional photo in your status updates. All you need to do is click the **Attach Photos** icon below the Status Update box and follow the on-screen cues and instructions prior to sharing your update. When you click Attach Photo, Facebook presents the following options:

- **Upload a Photo:** Click **Upload a Photo,** click **Browse,** select a photo stored on your computer, click **Open,** and Facebook uploads the photo for you.

- **Take a Photo:** Assuming your computer is equipped with a functioning webcam, click **Take a Photo,** click the little camera icon near the bottom of the photo preview area, strike a pose, and wait for Facebook to snap your picture. After you click the camera icon, a three-second on-screen countdown commences. When the camera icon reappears, Facebook is done snapping your mug shot. If you don't like the photo, click the **X** in the upper right of the photo and do your reshoot.

- **Create an Album:** Click **Create an Album,** click in the **Album Name** box, and type a name for the album. (Optionally, you can type a location and description for the album and use the Privacy settings to restrict access to the photos in this album.) Click **Create Album** and then follow the on-screen instructions to add photos to the new album.

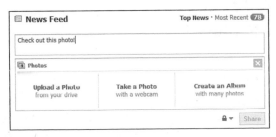

Facebook prompts you to upload a photo, take a photo with your webcam, or create a new photo album.

FRIEND-LY ADVICE

You can upload photos via e-mail! After clicking **Attach Photos, Upload a Photo,** click the **upload via email** link to obtain a special e-mail address where you can send photos to have them uploaded to Facebook. When you upload a photo via e-mail, it's posted to your News Feed as a status update and is visible to all of your friends. The subject line becomes the photo's caption. (In Chapter 7, you learn how to create albums and enter settings that enable you to control where your e-mail–uploaded photos are posted and who can view them.)

Attaching a Video

Everyone loves a good video, so if you're handy with a digital camcorder or love to record cameo appearances with your webcam, you
can easily upload your clips or record them directly to Facebook and
include them with your status updates.

Keep in mind that Facebook's policies restrict members to posting
only videos they or their friends have made. If you want to include
a video from somewhere else on the Internet, insert a link to it, as
explained later in this chapter.

To post a video, click **Attach Video,** click one of the following
options, and follow the on-screen cues and instructions to record or
upload the video clip you want to attach:

- **Record a Video:** To record a video using your webcam, click
  Record a Video, click the little red dot near the bottom of
  the photo preview area, wait for Facebook to start recording,
  and then do your thing. When you're done, click the red button again to stop recording. If you don't like the video, click
  the **X** in the upper right of the video and repeat the steps to
  "Take two!"

- **Upload a Video:** If you already have a video clip stored on
  your computer, click **Upload a Video,** click **Browse,** select a
  video file stored on your computer, click **Open,** and Facebook
  will upload the video for you. This can take some time,
  depending on the size of the file and your connection speed.

Posting an Event

When you're planning a get-together, making phone calls and sending
out invitations can be a royal hassle. If everyone you want to invite is
on Facebook, invitations are a snap. You just compose a status update,
click the **Attach Event** button, enter the event details (what, where,
and when), and click **Share.** For specifics on how to use the Event feature, check out Chapter 11.

Inserting a Link

To call attention to web content outside your News Feed, you can easily post a link to it. Your friends can then click the link to check out the web page for themselves.

Before you share a link, make sure you have the right address of the page you want to link to. Open that page in your browser window, click in the **Address** box to highlight the page's address, and then press the keystroke you use to copy stuff. You can now share the link.

At the bottom of the Publisher, click **Attach Link.** The Link form appears. Click in the **http://** box and type or paste the web page address you copied. (You don't need to type http:// at the beginning of the address.) Click **Attach.** Facebook attaches the link along with a portion of the first sentence from the source page. If the page contains photos or images, you'll be prompted to select a thumbnail image representative of the link. Use the arrow buttons to select the thumbnail you want, or click **No Thumbnail.** Type something in the text box if you want to, then click **Share.**

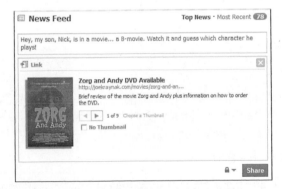

You can link to web pages from the Publisher.

Adding Other Stuff

In addition to photos, videos, events, and links, Facebook allows you to attach and post other stuff, depending on the applications you use. To attach other items, click the **More** button (if available), choose the item you want to attach, and enter any required settings as prompted.

Keep in mind that what you can attach (what's listed in the More menu) is limited to standard Facebook features plus other applications you've chosen to install. For more about Facebook applications, see Part 3.

Responding to a Friend's Post

When a friend posts something to his Wall or News Feed, it typically appears in your News Feed, unless your friend kept you out of the loop (by limiting how much of his information you can see via his privacy settings). You can then read the update, post a comment on it, "like" it (give it the thumbs up), and even share the update with your other friends.

Posting a Comment

The most common response to a friend's status update, other than ignoring it completely or just reading it, is to comment on it. Click the **Comment** link just below the message, type your comment in the box that appears, and click the **Comment** button.

WHOA!

Whatever you write as a comment will be viewable by all of your friend's Facebook friends as well as all your friends. If your comment is of a highly personal nature, take a minute to think it through before commenting in public, and consider sending your thoughts with a Facebook message instead. See Chapter 5 for more about Facebook's Message feature.

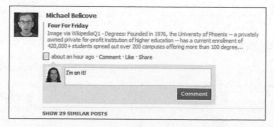

You can easily comment on a friend's post.

Voting Your Approval

Even easier than posting a comment is to express your approval of what your friend posted. All you need to do is click the **Like** link just below the post. A little thumbs-up icon appears, along with your username, indicating your vote of approval. Another way to respond to a friend's post is to share it with your friends by posting it to your News Feed or sending it via a message to one or more friends. Click the **Share** link below the post. Type a brief message introducing the item you're reposting and indicating why you think it's noteworthy. To repost the item, click **Share.** To send it as a message, click **Send as a Message** instead (lower left) and then click the **Send Message** button.

Hiding a Friend's Status Updates

When a friend is monopolizing the conversation on your Wall or News Feed by posting too much content that doesn't really interest you, you can easily hide that person's posts:

1. Click **Home** to display your News Feed, and click **Most Recent** (above your News Feed).

2. Rest the mouse pointer over a post from the friend whose updates you want to hide, and click **Hide** (to the right of the post's title).

3. Click **Hide** followed by your friend's name. Poof! The person's status updates magically disappear from your News Feed and Wall.

You can hide a friend's status updates.

To hide something other than a status update, such as a game that one or more of your friends likes to play, hover the mouse pointer over any post that contains the content you want to hide, click **Hide** (to the right of the post's title), and then click **Hide** followed by the content you want to hide, such as **Hide FarmVille.**

You can unhide posts from friends and content you've chosen to hide. Scroll to the bottom of the News Feed and click **Edit Options.** The Hidden from News Feed dialog box appears. Click the **Friends or Applications** button for the options you want to add back into your News Feed, and then click the **Add to News Feed** button next to the item you want to unhide.

You can add hidden content back into your News Feed.

Posting to a Friend's Wall

Assuming your friend allows friends to post to her Wall and hasn't specifically blocked you from doing so, you can write on your friend's Wall by posting a message or comment. Whatever you post can be seen not only by your friend but also by any of your friend's friends who happen to click by. It will also appear in your mutual friends' News Feeds.

To post to your friend's Wall, first head there by clicking your friend's name or photo. You can then proceed to do one of the following:

- Click in the **Write something ...** box, type your message, attach something if you like, and click **Share.**

- Click the **Comment** link below any of your friend's posts, type a comment, and click **Comment.**

Checking a Wall-to-Wall Discussion

Whenever two Facebook friends post to one another's Walls, they're engaging in a Wall-to-Wall discussion. As long as both parties are your friends or one of the parties is you, you can view the Wall-to-Wall discussion. To do so, click **See Wall-to-Wall** below the status update (in your News Feed or on your Wall or a friend's Wall).

Click See Wall-to-Wall

You can follow Wall-to-Wall discussions between friends.

If the discussion doesn't include you, you can still comment on or "Like" one of your friend's status updates, but you can't post a comment of your own. If you're involved in the Wall-to-Wall discussion, you can post a comment or a follow-up post, which then appears on your Wall and on the Wall of the friend who's engaged in the Wall-to-Wall with you.

Wishing a Friend a Happy Birthday

Most people, unless they're hard-core curmudgeons or would rather be dead, appreciate receiving a birthday note, so if a friend's birthday is coming up, consider wishing them a happy birthday on Facebook. Facebook will even remind you! Even though it has over 400 million users, Facebook does a spectacular job of keeping track of everyone's birthday. In the column to the right of your News Feed, Facebook displays reminders of any of your friends' birthdays that are coming up soon.

To receive advance notification of upcoming friend's birthdays via e-mail, click **Account** in the top menu and then **Account Settings.** On the Account Settings page, click the **Notifications** tab, and under Facebook, select the e-mail option for "Has a birthday coming up." Each week you'll receive a concise e-mail from Facebook with information about your friends' upcoming birthdays.

Poking a Friend

On Facebook, you can poke or be poked. When you poke a friend, you're letting the person know you're thinking of her. She can then poke you back or simply ignore you.

To poke a friend, head to the person's Wall by clicking on his name or Profile image. On the left, just below the person's photo (or the space where the person's photo would normally appear), click the **Poke** link. This sends a Poke notification to your friend's Home page with the options to Remove Poke or Poke Back.

If someone is poking you incessantly and won't stop even after you ask them to, you can block the person, as explained in Chapter 6. You can disable poking notifications that show up in your e-mail Inbox on the Notifications tab in Account Settings.

To Share or Not To Share?

Sprinkled throughout Facebook and all over the web are links that enable you to share content with your friends on Facebook. You're likely to see the Facebook Share icon in all sorts of places—on web pages, blog posts, photo sites, video sites, and so on. To share something, you can click the **Facebook Share** link wherever you happen to see it and then follow the on-screen instructions to post it to your News Feed or e-mail it to your friends. From within Facebook, you can share your and your friends' photos, videos, notes, and anything else containing the Share icon.

On some sites, you may see a different type of Share icon that doesn't look like the Facebook Share icon, but it can still link you to Facebook Share. If you see a Share icon, try clicking it. It may open a menu that provides options for sharing the content on Facebook, Twitter, MySpace, and other social networks. You can proceed by clicking the **Facebook Share** icon.

The Facebook Share icon is popping up on sites all over the web.

After you click the **Facebook Share** icon, you're automatically transported to Facebook, where you can log in (if you're not already logged in) or complete the Post to Profile box. Type a message introducing the content you're about to share, then click the **Share** button.

WHOA!

Share with care. You can seriously damage or destroy a relationship by sharing content that a friend strongly disagrees with, finds offensive, or had no intention of having you share with others. When choosing material to share, consider avoiding hot-button issues like politics or religion. And never, ever pass along sensitive information that your friends shared with you in confidence. If you have any doubt about sharing something a friend posted, ask your friend before sharing it with others.

Notes, along with links, photos, videos, or posts from external blogs, also contain a Share link you can click to post it to your News Feed, thus sharing it with any friends who visit your Wall or receive your status updates.

To share a friend's note, picture, video, or link, click **Share** to display the Post to Profile dialog box. Type a message to briefly describe the item or explain why you're sharing it, then click the **Share** button. The item is posted on your Wall and in your News Feed, where your friends can check it out.

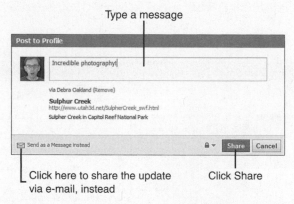

You can share a friend's post by posting it to your Profile, placing it on your Wall and in your News Feed.

The Least You Need to Know

- Your News Feed contains status updates and notifications of your friends' activities on Facebook. Your Wall contains a running display of your status updates along with comments and content added by friends followed by a list of your activities on Facebook.

- Posting a status update is easy. Click **What's on your mind?** in the Publisher and share away.

- You can post photos and videos by clicking on the appropriate icon in the bottom part of the Publisher.

- To comment on a friend's post, click the **Comment** link below the post.

- If you're compelled to share a friend's photo, video, or note, click the **Share** link under the item you wish to share.

Messaging ...
E-Mail, That Is

In This Chapter

- Navigating your way through your messages
- Fielding incoming messages
- Composing and sending messages
- Messaging to multiple Facebook friends all at once

After encountering the Wall, *messages* (Facebookese lingo for "e-mail") can seem kind of blasé, and it really is. However, some things are better said in private than plastered on a Wall for all to see, so Facebook provides its own internal e-mail system that enables friends to communicate in private.

Facebook may not be the best e-mail platform, but it does offer a few advantages. It allows you to send messages to Facebook members even if you don't know their e-mail addresses. You can also easily attach links, videos, photos, and Facebook gifts to your outgoing messages and follow discussion threads that develop as you carry on e-mail conversations among multiple Facebook friends.

Assuming you've used some sort of e-mail program (and we do assume you have), getting up to speed with Facebook's messaging system will be a snap. In this chapter, we cover the basics and point out a few special features that you won't find in just any old e-mail program.

Accessing Your Messages

Whenever you log in to Facebook, the top menu shows the number of messages you've received but haven't yet read. To view a list of recent messages, simply click the **Messages** icon. The Messages menu drops down, displaying several of your most recent messages with the newest message first.

To get to your main Messages area, click **See All Messages** (at the bottom of the menu). This takes you to a list of all messages you received—both those you have and haven't read. Unread messages are shaded a light blue; those you've already read are unshaded (like the page background). If you have more than one screen of messages, you can click the forward and back buttons above or below the list to view the next or previous screen.

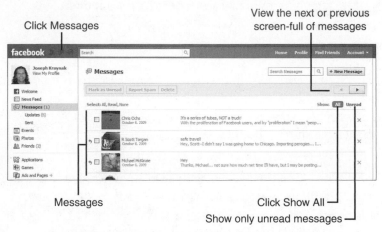

Click Messages

View the next or previous screen-full of messages

Messages

Click Show All

Show only unread messages

Your Messages area displays a list of messages you received.

Just above the message list toward the right, you can click **Unread** to display only those messages you haven't yet opened. You can always switch back to the full listing by clicking **All.**

WHOA!

Facebook is a social-networking platform, *not* an e-mail program. Don't assume your recipients will appreciate hearing from you via Facebook messages, especially if they're used to communicating with you through your business or home e-mail account. Facebook messaging is great for direct communication with an individual, especially if what you have to say is unsuitable for a public post, but use it in moderation.

Incoming! Reading and Replying to New Messages

To read a message, click its subject line. (If you click the sender's name or photo, you access the person's Profile.) The contents of the message appear. You can then click the forward or back button just above or below the message to flip to the next or previous message.

The message appears and you can reply to it.

To reply to a message, click in the **Reply** box (below the message), type your reply, and click **Reply.** In addition to sending a message, you can attach a photo, video clip, or link, as explained later in this chapter.

If you received a message and replied to it, or you sent a message and the recipient replied, both the original message and response are shown; that way, you can follow the discussion thread without having to search for old messages to see what you or someone else said.

You can always return to the list of messages by clicking **Messages** in the navigation bar to the left of the message area or **Back To Messages** above the message.

Searching for Messages

Most e-mail programs provide plenty of tools for managing your messages. You can create separate folders; copy or move messages to specific folders; sort messages by sender, recipient, or date; flag messages; and more. Comparatively speaking, Facebook's messaging feature is limited. It allows you to search for messages, flag messages as read or unread, and delete threads to reduce the clutter.

You can search for messages by name (sender or recipient) or by keyword (to find all messages that mention the upcoming family reunion, for example). To search for a message, click in the **Search Messages** box, type a friend's name or a keyword or phrase, and click the **Search** button (the one with the magnifying glass on it).

 FRIEND-LY ADVICE

If you're typing a friend's name, you usually only need to type the first few letters. Facebook auto-completes the entry for you.

Facebook displays a list of all the messages that match your search entry. You can then click the message you want to read.

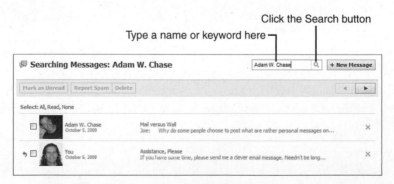

You can search for messages by name or keyword.

Selecting Messages

You probably noticed that to the left of every message in the Inbox is a checkbox. To select a message, so you can mark it as unread, delete it, or report it as spam, click the checkbox. You can click several checkboxes to select multiple messages. You can also click the following links above the message list to select or unselect an entire group of messages:

- **All:** Selects all the messages in your Inbox.

- **Read:** Selects only the messages you've already read.

- **None:** Deselects any selected messages.

Flagging Messages as Unread

As you open messages, presumably to read them, Facebook marks them as "read." This means the message no longer appears in the count of new messages that Facebook displays next to the Messages icon in the top menu. It also means you can click **Show: Unread** above the message list to filter out messages you've already read.

If a message is important, you may want to flag it as unread after reading it, so it doesn't get lost in the list. You can flag one or more messages as unread by taking the following steps:

1. Click the checkbox next to each message you want to flag as unread.

2. Click **Mark as Unread** in the bar above the message list.

Deleting Messages

When you're done with a particular message or discussion, you can easily delete it. Select the messages you want to delete and then click **Delete** in the bar above the message list.

WHOA!

Deleting a thread (discussion) deletes all messages in that discussion—so before you click that Delete button, make sure you really want everything in that thread deleted.

Reporting Spam

Facebook's setup is not prone to spam, but spammers are known to bend and break the rules. As a result, you may become the unfortunate recipient of Facebook e-mail spam. If you do receive spam, report it to Facebook so management can crack down on the perpetrators.

To report spam, select the spam messages and, in the toolbar above the message list, click **Report Spam.**

Checking for Updates

Any Facebook Group, Event, or page you join automatically messages you whenever an administrator of one of those areas posts an update. To check for updates, click **Updates** in the left menu (below Messages). You can always unsubscribe from a Group, Event, or page to stop receiving updates. Just click the checkbox next to any update you received from that Group, Event, or page and then click the **Unsubscribe** button in the bar above the updates. You can always resubscribe by using the Edit Subscriptions button below the list of updates.

Outgoing! Sending Messages

Usually, you have to send mail to get mail, so if you want a Messages list brimming with messages from your Facebook friends, start composing and sending messages. In the following sections, we show you how to compose a new message to send to an individual or to multiple recipients, whether the person is your Facebook friend or not.

Sending a New Message to a Facebook Member

Composing and sending a message in Facebook is a snap. Click the **Messages** icon in the top menu and click **Send a New Message** or, if the Messages screen is already displayed, click **+ New Message** (upper right). The Compose Message dialog box appears.

Now do the same thing you usually do when sending e-mail: address the message, type a description in the Subject box and a message in the Message box, and click **Send.** The only variation is when you're addressing your message. Instead of typing an e-mail address, click in the **To** box and type a friend's name. (As you start typing, Facebook displays the names of friends that match what you typed so far. You can click a name to add it to the To box.)

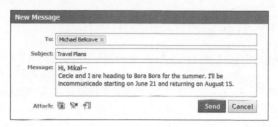

Send a message.

You can usually contact a person via Facebook messaging through the person's Profile, even if the individual is not a Facebook friend. To do so, go to the person's Profile and click **Send ... a Message** (below the person's Profile photo). Complete the message form and click **Send.**

POKE

You may not be able to e-mail Facebook members who are not your friends. Facebook gives members the option to hide the Send ... a Message link on the limited Profile that appears in a search.

Sending a Message to an Address Outside Facebook

You can send messages to e-mail addresses outside Facebook, regardless of whether the recipient is a Facebook member, by typing the person's e-mail address, instead of a friend's name, into the **To** box. Before you e-mail outside Facebook, note the following.

- Non-Facebook members can receive your messages, but they can't just click Reply to respond to your message. To reply, they can click a link inside the message that opens a Facebook page in the person's web browser prompting the person to join Facebook.

- Don't spam from Facebook. If someone complains, you may have your Facebook account cancelled.

Sharing Photos, Videos, or Links

Just as you can post a photo, video, or link to your News Feed or Wall, you can attach these items to outgoing Facebook messages. When composing a message, click one of the following links and then follow the on-screen cues to complete the operation:

- **Photo:** To attach a digital photo stored on your computer or snap a photo using a webcam.

- **Video:** To attach a recorded video clip stored on your computer or shoot footage on the fly with a webcam.

- **Link:** To attach a link to the message that the recipient can click to pull up a web page or blog. (If you type or paste a web page address starting with http:// into the body of your message, Facebook automatically displays a box for attaching a link to the outgoing message.)

For details about working with photos, check out Chapter 7. For details on working with video, visit Chapter 8.

Mass Mailing to Multiple Recipients

You can send the same message to several recipients with a single click of a button by entering a friend list or multiple friends' names and/or e-mail addresses in the **To** box. (See Chapter 3 for instructions on how to create a friend list.)

Well, that was easy. The tricky part is when you're carrying on an e-mail discussion with multiple friends. If someone replies to your message and sends the reply to the entire group, you have the option to reply to the entire group or to that particular individual:

- To reply to the group, type your message in the **Reply** box and click the **Reply** button.

- To reply to the individual only, click the person's name or e-mail address, type your message in the **Reply** box, and click the **Reply** button. This creates a *branched thread* in which you and the other person can carry on a discussion outside the main discussion.

> **WHOA!**
>
> Be careful who you're replying to. Facebook members have been known to mistakenly send a reply to the entire group, thinking they were replying only to a particular individual. If the message contains something embarrassing or insulting to one of the people in the group, you could have a lot of explaining to do and apologies to make.

Reviewing Messages You Sent

As you send messages, Facebook stores them in your Sent folder. To get to those messages, click **Sent** in the left menu. Except for the actual messages in the list, the display is identical to the Messages screen, so navigating your Sent folder and managing the messages in it should be familiar to you at this point.

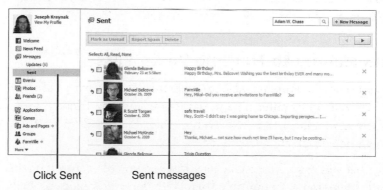

Click Sent   Sent messages

Facebook stores copies of messages you send in the Sent folder.

Taking Notice of Notifications

Unless you specify otherwise (via your account settings, as explained in Chapter 1), you will receive notifications whenever anything notable occurs on Facebook that involves you—whenever someone sends you a message, adds you as a friend, confirms your friend request, tags you in a photo, tags one of your photos, invites you to join a group, and so on.

To view recent notifications, click the **Notifications** icon (left end of the top menu). To view all Notifications, click the **Notifications** icon and then click **See All Notifications.** Each notification contains one or more links you can click to instantly jump to the area where the activity took place or to the Profile of the person responsible. Separate links may appear so close together that they look like a single link; mouse over the link(s), and it'll be clear whether you're dealing with one or more.

Facebook also forwards the notification to the e-mail address you used to register on Facebook (unless you have modified the setting), to your instant messaging account, and/or to your cell phone or other mobile device if you're using Facebook mobile (see Chapter 15). To subscribe to notifications via text message or *RSS* feed, click the **Notifications** icon, click **See All Notifications,** and then use the links under Subscribe to Notifications to set up your subscription(s). If you choose to subscribe via RSS feed, Facebook displays your notifications feed page which contains a Subscribe to this feed link. Click the link and follow the instructions to add the feed to your web browser.

DEFINITION

RSS (Really Simple Syndication) is a technology that automatically pulls together entries and displays them on a web-based or desktop RSS reader for quick access.

The Least You Need to Know

- To access Facebook's messaging platform, click **Messages** in the top menu and then click **See All Messages.**

- Composing and sending messages to Facebook friends is similar to e-mailing from your normal e-mail program. Click the **Messages** icon and then click **Send a New Message** or click the **+ New Message** button on the Messages screen and do the usual e-mail thing.

- You can send messages to people who are not Facebook members by typing their e-mail address into the **To** box.

- Click the **Photo, Video,** or **Link** icons at the bottom of the Compose Message dialog box to attach one of these items to an outgoing message.

- To send the same message to several Facebook friends, type each friend's name into the **To** field in the Compose Message dialog box.

Protecting Your Privacy and Profile

In This Chapter

- Restricting access to your personal information
- Banning certain members from contacting you
- Protecting yourself from phishers, hackers, spammers, and other low-lifes
- Keeping your e-mail address from falling into the wrong hands

One of the coolest features of Facebook is that it gives you a great deal of control over what others see. You can restrict access to information contained in your Profile, including contact information and where you work or attend school. You also control who can search for you and what they see when they find you, access to certain photo albums, and the information available to applications you use on Facebook.

Before you bare your soul on Facebook, you should be aware of just how private and secure your information is likely to be and any threats that might be lurking on or beyond your Wall. This chapter discusses key privacy and security concerns and shows you how to protect yourself and any sensitive information on Facebook.

Setting Your Privacy Preferences

Although Facebook is open to the public, your life doesn't need to be. Facebook provides privacy settings you can use to restrict or allow access to your information and activities on Facebook. By default, only your Facebook friends have access to most of your Profile information and can see your status updates and various activities you engage in.

In addition, Facebook *never* discloses pokes (except to the person you poke), messages (except to the recipient), whose Profile or photos you view, whose notes you read, groups and events you decline to join, friend requests you ignore or reject, friends you remove, or notes and photos you delete.

WHOA!

Facebook's privacy features are not foolproof. Even if you employ all measures to tighten security, your status updates, photos, videos, and any other information you place on Facebook could fall into the wrong hands and come back to haunt you. People have lost jobs and attracted the attention of law enforcement for what they've posted on Facebook, so follow our advice and share with care.

To access your privacy settings, click **Account** (in the top menu) and click **Privacy Settings.** The Privacy page appears, presenting links for accessing four groups of privacy settings—Profile Information, Contact Information, Applications and Websites, and Search—along with Block List to prevent certain people from contacting you on Facebook. We cover these options in the following sections.

Profile Privacy

To tighten or relax restrictions on who can view your Profile information, click **Profile Information** on the Privacy Settings page. This displays the Profile privacy page, which allows you to adjust your privacy settings for all sections of your Profile, including your About Me and Personal Information, and Education and Work, along with photos and videos in which you've been tagged, posts by you or your friends, and comments on posts. This page also includes an option you can uncheck to prevent friends from posting on your Wall, although we can't imagine why you'd want to prevent your friends from writing on your Wall.

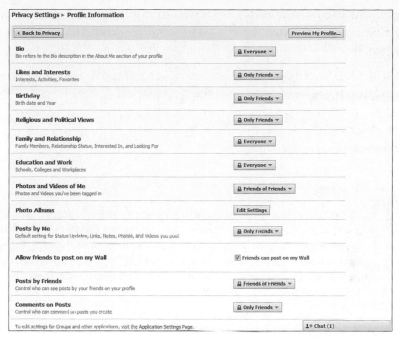

You can tighten or relax restrictions on access to specific information.

For most items on this page, you can enter preferences to restrict or open access to Everyone, Friends of Friends, or Only Friends. Most items also include a Customize option with additional choices:

- **Specific people:** If you choose this option, a text box appears, prompting you to type the names of friends or one or more of your friend lists you're allowing to access this content.

- **Only me:** Blocks access to everyone but you.

- **Hide this from:** You can choose Friends of Friends or Only Friends and then exclude individuals or the people on one or more of your friend lists by entering them in this text box.

When you're done entering your preferences in the Custom Privacy dialog box, click **Save Setting.**

If you don't want friends posting to your Wall, scroll down to Allow friends to post on my Wall and click the checkbox next to **Friends can post on my Wall,** removing the checkmark. You can also control access to your photo albums by clicking the **Edit Settings** button across from Photo Albums. (More about this in Chapter 7.)

Contact Information Privacy

By default, only friends have access to most of the contact information you've entered, including your instant messaging address(es), phone number(s), and home address. However, you can tighten or loosen restrictions on this information. Click **Contact Information** and enter your preferences. Although the list of items is different, use the same approach described in the previous section to change your preferences for each item.

> **WHOA!**
>
> We discourage you from providing access to your e-mail address, even to your Facebook friends. If a hacker obtains your e-mail address, he has half the information he needs to log in to your account and all the information he needs to start spamming you. If you keep your e-mail address hidden, people can contact you by sending you a Facebook message. Then if you want them to have your direct e-mail address, you can e-mail it to them.

Wondering what your friend will see when he chooses to view your Profile? Click **Preview My Profile** (upper right on any of the privacy pages). Facebook displays your Profile as it appears to most people on Facebook. To see how your Profile appears to one of your friends, click in the **Start typing a friend's name** box, and then click your friend's name.

You can view your Profile as others will see it.

To return to the Privacy Settings page, click **Back to Privacy Settings** (upper right).

Applications and Websites Privacy

Certain applications and websites require access to your Profile information to do whatever it is they do. Here's a summary of the types of information Facebook gives applications and websites access to and the activities that trigger these permissions:

- If you or one of your friends visits an application or Facebook-enhanced website, the application or website can access only the information in your public Profile—your name, networks, Profile picture, and friend list—plus any information you choose to make available to "everyone." (A Facebook-enhanced website is one that Facebook does not own or operate but that interfaces with the Facebook platform on a permission basis.)

- When you authorize an application (see Chapter 13), you give it permission to access any information in your account that it requires to work, except for your contact information.

- Facebook requires applications and websites to honor all of your privacy settings.

- If a friend authorizes an application, it can access any information in her account that it requires to work, including your friend's friend list—this means even if you don't authorize the application it has permission to access some of your information, too.

- If you visit a Facebook-enhanced website, it may access information in accordance with the previous rules in this list. If you choose not to proceed with a Facebook-related action on an external website, Facebook deletes any information about you that the site may have collected and sent back to Facebook.

You can restrict application access to some of your information by adjusting the application and website privacy settings. Head to the Privacy page and click **Applications and Websites.** Across from

What you share, you can click the **Learn More** button to access a brief explanation of the information that may be shared when you or a friend uses a Facebook application or a Facebook enhancement on an external website.

Privacy Settings ▸ Applications and Websites

◂ Back to Privacy

What you share
Learn about what you share when using applications and websites
[Learn More]

What your friends can share about you
Control what your friends can share about you when using applications and websites
[Edit Settings]

Blocked Applications
Block specific applications from accessing your information and contacting you
[Edit Blocked Applications]

Ignore Application Invites
Ignore application invites from specific friends
[Edit Ignored Friends]

Activity on Applications and Games Dashboards
Control who can see your activity in the Friends' Recent Activity, Friends' Applications and Friends' Games sections of these pages
[🔒 Only Friends ▾]

Instant Personalization
Control how select partners can personalize their features with my public information when I first arrive on their websites
[Edit Setting]

You can restrict application access to your information.

On the Applications and Websites privacy page, you can change the privacy settings for the following options:

- **What your friends can share about you:** Your Facebook friends may share information about you with an application or Facebook-enhanced external website. For example, your friend may use a greeting card application that gathers the names and birthdays of all her friends to prompt her to send a card on her friend's birthday. To prevent your friends from sharing certain pieces of information about you, click **Edit Settings** and remove the checkbox next to every piece of information you *don't* want your friends passing along.

- **Blocked Applications:** If you blocked any Facebook applications from accessing your information and contacting you, you can click Edit Blocked Applications to display a screen that enables you to unblock each one. For instructions on how to block a Facebook application, check out Chapter 13.

- **Ignore Application Invites:** If you're receiving unsolicited and unappreciated invitations to use applications from one or more friends, you can block initiations from them. Click

Edit Ignored Friends, start typing the friend's name, and click the name when Facebook displays the full version. You can also use this screen to remove friends from this blacklist. See Chapter 13 for an easier way to add friends to the list.

- **Activity on Applications and Games Dashboards:** When you and a friend play the same game or use the same application, your activities in these games or applications may show up on one another's accounts so, for example, your activities may show up on your friend's account where his friends can see what you're up to. To control access to this information, click the button across from this option and click **Only Friends, Everyone,** or **Friends of Friends,** or click **Customize,** use the Custom Privacy dialog box to enter your preferences, and then click **Save Setting.**

- **Instant Personalization:** Unless you specify otherwise, Facebook partner websites can use your public information to personalize the features it offers on its website. To prevent this, click the **Edit Setting** button and then remove the checkmark next to the Allow option.

Search Privacy

You can hide on Facebook so nobody can find you—or only your friends and perhaps their friends can find you—when searching for you by name. That sort of defeats the purpose of Facebook as a networking tool, but hiding is an option. Facebook also allows you to control how much information nonfriends can access when they do find you by performing a search.

To adjust your privacy settings for a search, go to the Privacy Settings page, and click **Search.** The search-privacy page appears, displaying only two options:

- **Facebook Search Results:** By default, your name can come up in the search results of Everyone (all Facebook members). To limit this to only friends or friends of friends, click the button across from Facebook Search Results and click the desired option.

• **Public Search Results:** By default, search engines can index your Profile and any information you choose to share with everyone. To block search engine access to your information, remove the checkmark from the Allow checkbox.

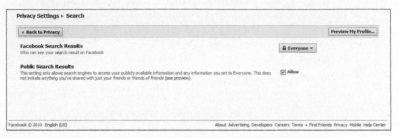

You can limit who can find you on and off Facebook.

Blocking Annoying Individuals

When someone becomes more of a nuisance than a true friend, you may want to block the person entirely. A block prevents the person from viewing your Profile and severs all ties, including friendship connections and friend details. In addition, your Profile won't appear in his searches, and his Profile won't appear in yours. That'll teach him!

WHOA!

Removing someone from your blocked list does not automatically restore your friendship. If you want to take the person back as a friend, you'll need to send him a new friend request and grovel for his approval, as discussed in Chapter 3.

The easiest way to block someone is to go to the Privacy Settings page, click **Block List,** click in the **Person** box, type his name, and click **Block.** Facebook blocks the person but does not notify the person of the block, because that would be downright rude. (You can block a person by e-mail address, instead, which comes in handy if the person isn't a Facebook member. Just use the Email box instead of the Person box.)

If the person you want to block is not on your friend list, you have another way to block her. Pull up her Profile and click the **Report/ Block this Person** link (near the bottom of the left column, last time we looked). The **Report and/or block ...** dialog box appears, and you can choose to block the person, report the individual (be sure to select a reason), or both. (To block or report a friend, first de-friend the individual, as explained in Chapter 3.)

You can block or report someone who's not a friend.

Defending Yourself from Hackers and Phishers

Facebook does a fairly good job of policing activity and cracking down on inappropriate behavior, but hackers, stalkers, schemers, and scammers have been known to ply their trade on the platform. To protect yourself, your information, and your account from these miscreants, you should be aware of the potential threats and practice some safe Facebooking strategies.

Keeping Hackers from Hijacking Your Account

A malicious hacker may be able to hijack your Facebook account and then pose as you. Once they gain access, they can do anything from posting tasteless jokes in your News Feed to e-mailing your friends requesting a money transfer or credit card information so you can fly back home from Bora Bora, where you've been robbed and held captive for 36 hours.

To protect your account and information from hackers, consider practicing the following safeguards:

- Change your password to something that's difficult for hackers to guess. Include both letters and numbers, and make it fairly long—10 to 14 characters is better than 6 to 8. Use a different password than you use for other online accounts. Remember, passwords are case sensitive. To access the form for changing your password, click **Account** (in the top menu), **Account Settings,** and then, across from Password, click **Change.**

- Change your password every three months or so.

- If other people have access to the computer you use to log in to Facebook, log out whenever you're done using Facebook. Also, don't use your browser's "remember" feature to store your username and password.

- Include as little sensitive information as possible in your Profile; if a hacker does gain access, he won't have your name, address, phone number, and other potentially sensitive information.

- Don't give your login information to anyone for any reason. Hackers may pose as Facebook representatives to trick you into passing along your login information. See the next section, "Dodging Phishing Schemes," for details.

- Download only programs you fully trust. Hackers can embed code in an otherwise harmless application that captures the keystrokes you press to log in and sends those keystrokes to the hacker.

- Add a security question to your account, so if it does get hijacked, you'll have an easier time regaining access to it. To access the form for adding or changing a security question, click **Account** (in the top menu), click **Account Settings,** and then click **Security Question.** (After you enter your security question, this option disappears and is no longer available—so if you don't see it, that's probably what happened.)

FRIEND-LY ADVICE

If your account has been hacked, try logging in to Facebook and changing your password. If the hacker already changed your password so you can't log in, go to www.Facebook.com, click the **Forgot your password?** link, and follow the on-screen instructions to try to reset your password. If that doesn't work, visit the Facebook Security page (facebook.com/security) for more information.

Dodging Phishing Schemes

Phishing scams dangle a line in front of you, hoping you'll take the bait. In this case, the bait is usually an e-mail alert warning you of some problem with your account. The alert usually contains a link you can click to go to a site where you can learn more and address the issue. The site typically looks official and matches what you expect to see—in this case, a Facebook-like interface. You think you're on Facebook, but you're really on a website the phisher created, and, before you can fix the problem, you have to log in.

Unfortunately, if you do try to log in, you pass your Facebook login information directly to the phisher, who can then log in to your real Facebook account, change your password, access your Profile information, pose as you, and cause all sorts of trouble.

To defend yourself against phishing schemes, practice the following maneuvers:

- Trust your instincts. If something looks or sounds a little phishy, it probably is.

- Keep in mind that just because something appears to be coming from a friend, it may not be. Your friend's account may have been hijacked.

- Compare the URL in the link with the one that appears in your browser or e-mail program's status bar when you rest the mouse pointer on the link. The link may show www.facebook.com but take you to an entirely different site. You can tell where a link is really going to take you by hovering the mouse pointer over the link and looking in the status bar.

- Keep in mind that Facebook will never ask for your login information. If someone's asking for it, they're probably bad guys.

- If it looks as though someone has hijacked a friend's account and is posing as him, contact your friend immediately.

- Report any suspected phishing scams to Facebook so management can investigate and shut down the perpetrators. At the top of every e-mail message you receive is a Report link you can click to report the suspicious message to Facebook. More details about reporting Facebook violations are provided later in this chapter.

Preventing and Stopping Spam

We haven't seen a great deal of spam on Facebook, probably because the service and its members do such a fine job of policing members and advertisers. If you do receive an e-mail message that appears to be spam, click the **Report Spam** link above the message and follow the on-screen instructions to report the spammer.

Keep in mind that if you're receiving spam that has supposedly originated from a Facebook friend, your friend's account probably has been hijacked. You can reduce your exposure to receiving spam from nonfriends by editing your Contact Information privacy settings to remove the link for sending you a message from your search Profile. Click the button across from Send me a message and click **Only Friends** or **Friends of Friends.** Only your friends (or your friends and their friends) will be able to see the link for sending you an e-mail message.

Reporting Scams and Schemes to Facebook

Facebook monitors members and the activities they engage in, but it relies on members like you to call attention to any abuse of the service. If you notice any lewd, crude, or potentially criminal activity on Facebook, report it. Following are various ways to file a report:

- **Click a Report link and follow the on-screen instructions.** Facebook displays the Report link in various places, including below the Profiles of members who are not your friends, above any open messages, above photos, in notes, and in groups.

- **E-mail abuse@facebook.com.** You can send an e-mail message to Facebook to report suspected member violations.

- **E-mail advertise@facebook.com.** Send an e-mail message to report any suspected abuse by advertisers on Facebook.

When notifying Facebook of suspected violations, be as specific as possible. Identify the member or advertiser by name and describe the violation and where you observed it.

A Word to Parents ...

Kids love Facebook almost as much as they love their cell phones—maybe more. Unfortunately, some kids are too naïve, and others too worldly, for their own good. Therefore, parents need to lay down the rules and enforce them to keep children out of harm's way.

Review Facebook's safety advice with your child. Click **Account, Help Center** (in the top menu) and then click the **Safety** tab (left menu). You may want to work through this chapter with your child to make sure you've reviewed the privacy preferences and adjusted them to your comfort level.

Following are some words of wisdom to share with your teenager (kids under 13 are not allowed to join Facebook—unless they lie about their age):

- Don't post your phone number, home address, school name, or any other information a stranger could use to track you down. Facebook's privacy features may not fully protect this information, so don't add it to your Profile.

- Don't friend strangers. Friend only people you already know and trust from your real-world encounters.

- Don't agree to face-to-face meetings with people you don't already know and trust in the real world.

- Don't believe everything a person says about himself in his Profile or otherwise. On the Internet, a 50-year-old child abuser can pass himself off as a 17-year-old Romeo.

- Report any inappropriate content or communications to your parents and to Facebook at abuse@facebook.com.

> **WHOA!**
>
> You can install computer nanny software to provide some level of protection, but no system is failsafe. Place the family computer(s) in a common area, where you can supervise your kids' computer use without seeming like you're hovering. Limit computer use to normal hours when you're awake and alert. Sticking a computer in a kid's room where they can loiter on Facebook 24/7 is neither healthy nor safe.

The Least You Need to Know

- Check and adjust your privacy settings—know what you're sharing, and restrict access to anything you don't want to share.

- To access the privacy settings, click **Account** and then click **Privacy Settings.**

- Consider removing your home address and phone number from your Profile and not sharing your e-mail address with anyone, especially if you're under the age of 18.

- Keep hackers at bay by using a password that's tough to guess and then changing it every three months or so.

- Never click a link in a message or post and then enter your username and password or other sensitive information, because you could fall victim to a phishing scam.

- Report any violations or suspicious activity to Facebook.

Getting More Involved with Facebook

Part 2

Although you establish and maintain relationships through Facebook, you also have a relationship with Facebook that develops over time as you get to know one another. The more Facebook knows about you and your friends, the better able it is to suggest new friends and present you with more relevant information. The more you know about Facebook, the better equipped you are to tap its full potential.

When you're ready to take your relationship with Facebook to the next level, we're ready to ramp you up. Here, we introduce you to one of the most popular features on Facebook—photo sharing—along with other features you may want to explore, including Groups, Chat, Events, and Notes. All of these features can enhance your experience on Facebook and the relationships you have with your Facebook friends.

Uploading and Sharing Photos

In This Chapter

- Viewing other people's photos
- Making photo albums to organize your photos
- Uploading quality photos on Facebook
- Tagging yourself and your friends in photos
- Limiting access to specific albums

Swapping photos online has become a favorite global pastime. With online photo-sharing services including Photobucket and Flickr, people can upload their photos and share them with anyone in the world who has a computer with Internet access.

Well, Facebook is in the photo-sharing business, too. All you have to do is create a photo album, upload your photos, and start sharing. This chapter shows you how and provides additional guidance on restricting photo access to only those people you want looking at them.

Looking at Photos

Chances are pretty good that if you've spent more than two minutes on Facebook, you've already seen a few photos. They show up in your News Feed, your Profile, your friends' Profiles, in groups, and in Facebook's Photo application.

- **News Feed:** If a friend posts a photo, a thumbnail version of it appears. You can click the photo to view a larger version and access any other photos in that album.

- **Your Profile:** Click **Profile** in the top menu and then click the **Photos** tab to check out your own photos.

- **Your friends' Profiles:** Click a friend's name or Profile photo and then click the **Photos** tab to check out your friend's photos.

- **Groups:** In the left menu (left of your News Feed that is), click the **Groups** icon, click a group you belong to, and then click one of the photos in the Photos section. This takes you to the Photos area, where group members can view and upload photos.

- **Photo application:** In the left menu, click **Photos.** The Photos page appears where you can view albums your friends have recently created or updated, photos uploaded using a mobile device, photos in which your friends have been tagged, your photos, and photos of you. Using the Photos application, you can also create your own albums, as explained in the following section.

You can access a friend's photos through his Profile.

POKE

Neither Photobucket nor Flickr can claim the top spot in the online photo-sharing arena. Facebook is the champ with over 3 billion photos uploaded to the site each month.

Preparing Photos for Uploading

After you've created an album, you can immediately begin *uploading* photos from your computer to the new album, but don't rush the process. First, make sure those photos are quality snapshots and then organize them into folders on your computer to simplify the upload process. The following sections show you how to properly prepare your photos for upload.

Editing Your Photos: Quality Counts

Too many Facebook members focus, snap, and upload—often skimping on the "focus" part. As a result, their albums are cluttered with lousy snapshots—too dark, too light, too much glare, weird colors, and so on. Prior to uploading your photos, use a photo-editing program to make them look as good as they possibly can be.

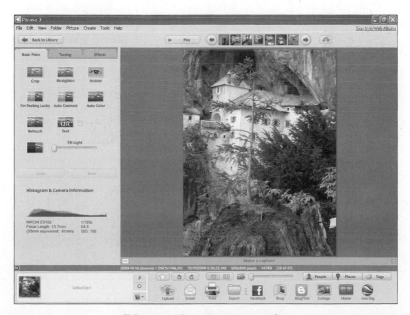

Edit your photos to ensure quality.

Most digital cameras and many printers come with their own photo-editing software. If you have no such program on your computer, consider uploading the photos to a different photo-sharing service first—one that has tools for editing your photos. You can then import your photos into Facebook as explained later in this chapter.

Organizing Photos into Folders

Whenever you *download* photos from your camera to your computer, store the photos in separate folders on your computer. Each folder can function as a separate album. This enables you to quickly upload an entire folder full of photos from your computer to one of your Facebook albums without having to select individual photos to include or exclude.

If you haven't organized the photos on your computer in separate folders, take some time and organize them now. We'll wait.

Uploading Photos

To make photos available on Facebook, you need to upload (copy) them from your computer or mobile device to Facebook. As with most tasks, Facebook offers more than one way to upload photos. In addition, you can use third-party applications that some Facebook members find faster and more convenient. In the following sections, you get to check out the various methods and choose the one you like best.

DEFINITION

Uploading and **downloading** are fancy words for *copying*. The direction, up or down, is relative to you. If you're copying something from somewhere else to the device you're using, you're downloading. If you're copying from the device you're using to somewhere else, you're uploading.

Uploading Photos to a New Album

To upload your photos to a new photo album using Facebook's Photo Uploader, here's what you do:

1. From your Home page, click **Photos** (left menu).

2. Click **+ Upload Photos** (upper right). The Add New Photos page appears with the Create Album tab up front.

3. Type an album name, location (geographical location of where you snapped the photos), or a brief description of the photos in the appropriate text boxes.

4. Open the **Privacy** list and choose who you want to have access to this album:

   • **Everyone:** Everyone on the Internet can view your photos, even people not logged in to Facebook.

   • **Friends of Friends:** Your friends and their friends can access the photos.

   • **Only Friends:** Only your friends can look at your photos.

   • **Customize:** Using this option, you can limit access to specific friends or friend lists.

5. Click **Create Album.** Facebook returns you to the Upload Photos page and prompts you to select photos stored on your computer to upload to the album. **Note:** The first time you create a photo album, Facebook attempts to install its Photo Uploader, but your browser may prompt you for confirmation. In Internet Explorer, for example, the Security bar pops up near the top of the window, and you must click it and then click the option to allow the installation to continue. Do whatever's necessary to bypass your browser's security and proceed with the installation.

6. Select the folder (on your computer) in which the photos are stored. Facebook displays thumbnail versions of the photos in the selected folder.

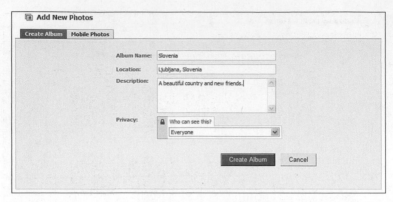

Create a new photo album.

7. (Optional) To rotate an image, mouse over it and then click the **Rotate Clockwise** or **Rotate Counterclockwise** icon that appears in either corner of the photo.

8. Take one of the following steps to select the photos you want to upload:

    • Click each individual photo to select it.

    • Click **Select All** to select all the photos in the folder.

    • Click **Select All** to select all the photos in the folder and then click each photo you don't want to upload to deselect it.

9. Click the **Upload** button. Photo Uploader starts uploading the photos to the selected album. This may take several minutes depending on the number of photos, their size and quality, and the speed of your Internet connection. When the upload is complete, Facebook displays a notification with a link to view the photos.

10. Click the link to view the photos you just uploaded.

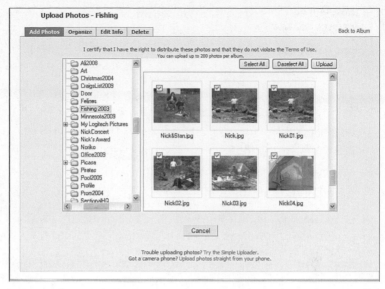

Use Facebook Photo Uploader to copy photos from your computer to a Facebook album.

Uploading Photos to an Existing Album

If you already have a photo album and want to add more photos to it, click **Profile** and then click the **Photos** tab. Click the album into which you want to upload more photos, and then click the **Add More Photos** link (just above the existing photos). This starts Facebook's Photos Uploader, which you can use to upload additional photos as explained in the previous section starting with Step 6.

To find out how to upload photos from your cell phone or other mobile device, head to Chapter 15.

Editing Your Photos and Albums

After uploading photos to an album on Facebook, you can edit the album or the photos it contains to add information about each photo, rearrange the photos in the album, delete photos, and much more.

To get started, click **Profile,** click your **Photos** tab, mouse over the album you want to work with, and click the **Edit Album** link in the upper-right corner of the album. This displays a screen with the following five tabs:

- **Edit Photos:** You can add a caption for each photo, tag people in the photo, and select which photo you want Facebook to use as the album cover. (More about these options in the following two sections.)

- **Add More:** Displays the Photo Uploader, which you can use to add photos to this album.

- **Organize:** Displays thumbnail versions of all the photos, which you can drag around to rearrange.

- **Edit Info:** Displays the album name, location, description, and privacy settings, so you can edit them.

- **Delete:** Deletes the entire album and its contents.

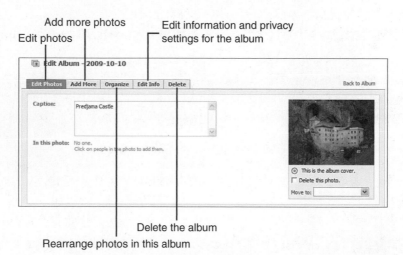

You can customize the album and the photos it contains.

Working on Individual Photos

You can do a great deal of customizing in the Edit Photos page, but some options are unavailable unless you view an image on its own page. To view an image solo, click **Profile,** click your **Photos** tab, click the album that contains the image, and then click the image.

In this view, you can make many of the same changes you can make using the Edit Photos page, including adding a caption, tagging the photo, and deleting the photo. In addition, you can …

- **Comment on the photo.** Click in the **Write a comment** box, type your comment, and click **Comment.**

- **Rotate the photo 90 degrees clockwise or counterclockwise.** Click the **Counterclockwise Rotate** or **Clockwise Rotate** button. (These buttons look like curved arrows pointing either counterclockwise or clockwise.)

- **Share the photo.** To post the photo and your comment to your Wall, click **Share +** and then type whatever you want to say about the photo and click **Share;** to send it as an e-mail, click the **Send as a Message instead** link, type the name of the Facebook friend you want to send it to, type a message, and click **Send Message.**

- **Make the photo your Profile picture.** Click **Make Profile Picture.**

Tagging Photos

Facebook lets you tag photos (yours or your friends') to identify people in those photos. Anyone viewing the photo can then mouse over people shown in the photo to view the tag. Whenever you tag a photo, the action is recorded in your News Feed, so your friends will know when you've tagged yourself or one of them. If you tag one of your Facebook friends, Facebook sends the person a notice and posts it in the person's News Feed.

To tag a photo, here's what you do:

1. Display the photo you want to tag. You can display the photo on the Edit Photos tab or on its own page.

2. If you're viewing the photo on its own page, click **Tag This Photo** below and to the right of the photo. (If you're on the Edit Photos tab, you don't have the Tag This Photo option.

Instead, when you mouse over the thumbnail version of the photo, the mouse pointer morphs into crosshairs and you just click whatever you want to tag in the photo.)

3. Position the mouse pointer (crosshairs) over the center of the person's face for the most accurate placement of your tag and click. The Tag box appears, in which you can do one of the following:

   • Choose your Facebook friend's name from the list provided.

   • Click in the **Type any name or tag** box and start typing the name of the person or object. As you type, the list of friend names narrows to match what you've typed so far, and you can click a name in the list. If you're tagging a person (or object) who is not a Facebook friend, just finish typing the name. (You can add the person's e-mail address to invite him to join Facebook and see the photo you just tagged him in.)

4. Repeat steps 2 and 3 to tag other people and objects in the photo.

5. Click **Tag.**

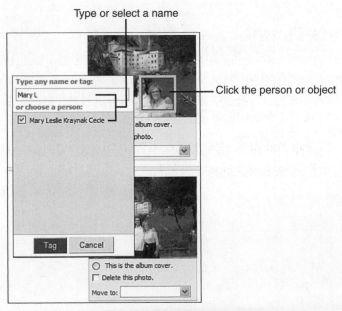

Tag yourself or your friends in photos.

NETIQUETTE

Some people don't appreciate being tagged in photos, particularly if they think the photo captured them in an unflattering light or embarrassing pose, so be careful. If a friend removes a tag or requests that you remove a photo, respect her wishes. If a friend keeps tagging you in photos and you want that to stop, send your friend a message asking her to cease and desist (diplomatically, of course). If she continues, consider de-friending her so she won't be able to tag you. For more about de-friending, check out Chapter 3.

You can remove a tag at any time. When you display a tagged photo, the tags appear below the photo. Next to the tag you want to remove, click **Remove tag.**

Rearranging Photos in Your Album

Unless you specify otherwise, Facebook displays the photos in an album in the order in which you uploaded them. You can rearrange the photos at any time. Here's how:

1. Click **Profile** in the top menu and then click the **Photos** tab. Your Photos page appears.

2. Click the album you want to rearrange. Facebook displays a page showing the photos in that album.

3. Click **Organize** (above the photos) to display the page for rearranging the photos.

4. Do one of the following:

    • Click **Reverse Order** to completely flip the order, displaying the last photo first and the first photo last.

    • Drag and drop the photos to manually rearrange them.

5. Click **Save Changes.**

Reverse the order   Drag and drop photos

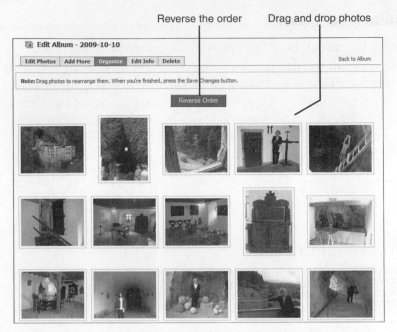

You can rearrange the photos in an album.

Managing Your Photos with Third-Party Applications

Facebook is actually ill-equipped to handle photos. Sure, you can upload photos and share them with your friends, but Facebook lacks the file-management and photo-editing tools present in dedicated photo-management services like Flickr and Picasa. As a result, you tend to see a lot of bad photos on Facebook—photos that are too dark, too light, have red-eye issues, and so on.

Because Facebook lacks the essential tools for managing photos, consider using a full-featured program or service and linking it to your Facebook account. Facebook includes applications for the most popular photo-sharing services, including Flickr and Picasa, which enable you to upload photos directly to Facebook. The following sections show you how.

Linking to Picasa

Google features an excellent photo-management program called *Picasa* that you can download (for free!) and use on your computer to manage your photos, edit them to look just right, and upload them into Picasa web folders (on Google). With the addition of the Picasa Uploader application for Facebook, you can edit the photos on your computer in Picasa and then upload them directly to your albums on Facebook—and even create new albums.

To learn more about Picasa, and download and install your free copy of the program, visit picasa.google.com.

After installing Picasa, take the following steps to install the Picasa Uploader for Facebook:

1. Close your web browser and restart it. Otherwise, if you try to install the Picasa plugin, Facebook will not recognize your recent Picasa installation and will not allow you to continue.

2. Go to apps.facebook.com/picasauploader.

3. Click **Install Now** and follow the on-screen instructions to complete the installation. This adds a button to Picasa that allows you to upload photos directly from Picasa to Facebook.

When you're ready to upload photos from Picasa to Facebook, select the photos in Picasa as you normally do and then click the **Facebook** button. The Facebook Uploader dialog box appears. Click **Start Upload.**

Select the images you want to upload

Click the Facebook button

You can upload photos directly from Picasa to Facebook.

Linking to Flickr

Yahoo!'s Flickr is the most popular service dedicated exclusively to digital photo sharing. Go to www.flickr.com, register for the service (it's free), and you can instantly begin uploading your photos. (To find additional tools for enhancing your Flickr experience, including the Flickr Uploadr for your desktop, visit www.flickr.com/tools.)

After you've uploaded some photos to your Flickr account, you can link your account to Facebook using an application like Flickr Importr:

1. Go to apps.facebook.com/flickrimportr. Facebook displays a confirmation screen asking whether you want to allow this application access to your information.

2. Click **Allow** and follow any additional on-screen instructions to complete the authentication.

To access Flickr Importr, click **Applications** (in the Applications bar) and click **Flickr Importr.**

POKE

Facebook has several applications available for importing photos from Flickr—and some are better than others. If Flickr Importr doesn't work for you, click **Applications, Browse More Applications,** and search for other Flickr applications. See Chapter 13 for more about hunting down Facebook applications.

With Flickr Importr, you simply click **Photos** to view thumbnails of the photos you have stored in your Flickr account. Click each photo you want to import into Facebook, and click **Submit.** You can then create a new Facebook album or add photos to an existing album and enter options for each photo. When you're done entering your preferences, click **Start Import.** Flickr Importr imports the photos from Flickr and places them in the specified album.

After importing the photos, open the album in which they're stored, select the photos, and then click the **Approve** button. You can then tag the photos, add captions, share the album, and so on.

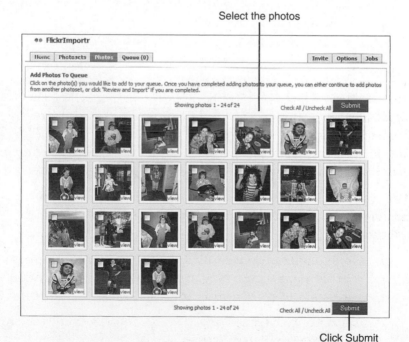

Flickr Importr can pull photos from Flickr into Facebook.

The Least You Need to Know

- To access your Photos page, click **Profile** (in the top menu) and then click your **Photos** tab.

- To create a photo album, click **Profile,** click your **Photos** tab, click **Create New Album,** and follow the on-screen cues.

- To view photos in one of your albums, click **Profile,** click the **Photos** tab, and click the album.

- Click a photo in your album to display it on a page of its own. From there, you can change the caption, add a comment, rotate the photo, tag people or objects shown in the photo, delete the photo, or make it your Profile photo.

- To tag yourself or a friend in a photo, click the photo to display it on its own page, click **Tag This Photo,** click the person, and then select the person's name from your friend list.

Uploading and Sharing Video Footage

In This Chapter

- Viewing your friends' video clips
- Adhering to Facebook's video guidelines
- Sharing your own video clips with friends
- Editing your video clips
- Getting personal with video e-mail

YouTube may be the leader in video hosting and sharing, but Facebook is no slouch in this arena. Members can upload video clips, post video clips on their Walls, tag and comment on clips, post notes with video, and even record footage directly to Facebook using a webcam!

Whether you're an indie filmmaker looking to spread the word about your new feature film or a proud parent wanting to share Junior's first steps with your extended family, this chapter helps you project your footage onto your Wall and share it in other areas in Facebook.

Viewing Other People's Video Clips

You don't have to fire up your camcorder to start enjoying Facebook's video features. If you have any filmmakers among your Facebook friends, you can watch their videos. In the following sections, we show you how to watch a video clip and comment on it, tag your-self or your Facebook friends in clips, and watch any videos in which you've been tagged.

Watching a Video Clip

Whenever one of your friends posts a video, it will appear in your News Feed letting you know, including a thumbnail of the video along with a play button. Click the **Play** button or anywhere on the thumbnail to run the video. Facebook enlarges the viewer and starts playing the clip.

Click the Play button

Click Play.

To check out whether one of your Facebook friends has recorded and uploaded any video, check out your friend's video page:

1. Head to your Profile page and in the left menu under Friends, click **See All.**

2. Click the name of the friend whose videos you want to view. This takes you to the person's Home page.

3. Click the **Video** tab. If your friend has no Video tab, your friend has no videos. If your friend has one or more videos, thumbnails of the videos appear.

4. Click the video you want to watch. Facebook displays the video on its own page.

5. Click the video to start playing it.

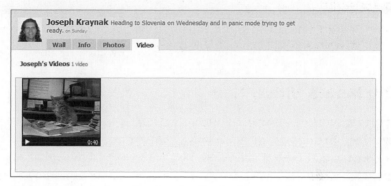

*Click the **Video** tab to view thumbnails of videos your friend has uploaded.*

To see recent video clips your friends have posted or have been tagged in all in one central location, head to your Video page. To get there from your Home page, click **Photos** (in the left menu) and then click **Video.**

Commenting on a Video Clip

Wherever you happen to find a video, you'll find a **Write a comment ...** box. Click inside the box, type your comment, and click **Comment.**

You can always delete one of your own comments by clicking **Delete** next to your comment.

Tagging a Video Clip

If a video includes cameo appearances of you or your friends, consider tagging the video to let people know who's in it. When you tag a video, the name of the person you tagged appears below it, and Facebook notifies your friend that he's been tagged. If you tag yourself, that recent activity may appear in your News Feed to keep your friends posted.

WHOA!

You can't undo a tag unless you're tagging yourself. As soon as you click the name of a Facebook friend to tag, the tag is applied to the video, and you can't remove it. Only the owner of the video and the person you tagged are authorized to remove the tag. So be sure the person you're tagging will want to be tagged!

To tag a video, first display it on its own page (by clicking on it). Click **Tag This Video,** and then start typing the name of a Facebook friend who appears in the video. As you type, the list of friend names narrows to match what you've typed so far, and you can click a name in the list. To enter another name, press **Enter** or **Return** and then enter the next name. When you're done, click **Done Tagging.**

Watching Videos in Which You've Been Tagged

Turnabout is fair play. Just as you can tag your Facebook friends in videos, they can tag you. If you do happen to get tagged, Facebook sends you a notification so you can check out the video. To view all the videos in which you've been tagged, take the following steps:

1. Click **Profile** icon (in the top menu bar). Facebook displays your Profile.

2. Click **Videos of Me** (below your Profile photo). If you don't see a Videos of Me link, nobody has tagged you in a video. If you've been tagged in any videos, the videos appear.

3. Click a video to display it on its own page.

4. Click the video to play it.

You can de-tag yourself by displaying the video on its own page and then clicking **Remove Tag.**

Click Videos of Me

You can view all videos in which you've been tagged.

Recording and Uploading Video Footage

With a digital camcorder or a webcam, you have all the equipment you need to shoot your own video footage. With Facebook's assistance, you can then upload your video to the web and share it with your friends.

In the following sections, we briefly explain Facebook's video guidelines and then show you how to access your Video page, upload video clips stored on your computer, record videos with a webcam, and then edit some of the details related to your clip.

Taking Note of Facebook's Video Guidelines

Facebook isn't YouTube. You can't just upload any video footage you think is cool. To keep the spotlight focused on friends, Facebook stipulates that any video clips you choose to upload and share meet the following conditions:

- Compliant with the Facebook Code of Conduct and Terms of Use. The term of use Facebook probably had in mind here is this one: "You will not post content that is hateful, threatening, pornographic, or that contains nudity or graphic or gratuitous violence."

- Personal in nature: Videos must be of you or your friends, taken by you or your friends, or original art or animation created by you or your friends.

- Does not infringe upon or violate the copyright, trademark, publicity, privacy, or other rights of any third party.

- Does not attempt to circumvent any filtering techniques or technologies Facebook may use to screen content.

WHOA!

If you post video that does not adhere to every single one of these guidelines, Facebook may remove the content and perhaps even terminate your account.

Accessing the Video Page

Facebook features everything you need to upload and share video, and all the tools are accessible via the Create a New Video page. To get to there from your Home page, click **Photos** (in the left menu), and then click the **+ Upload Video** button above the photos. The Create a New Video page appears.

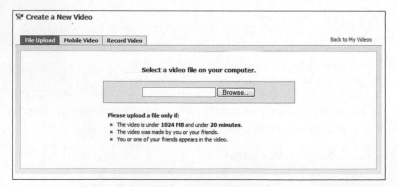

You can record and upload video via the Create a New Video page.

FRIEND-LY ADVICE

Create a Video tab for your Profile. Click **Profile** (in the top menu) to display your Profile. Click the **+** tab and click **Video.** You can now view your video library at any time by heading to your Profile and clicking the **Video** tab. In the upper-right corner of the Video page are buttons to Upload and Record video.

Uploading a Video Clip from Your Computer

If you have any digital video clips lying around on your computer, you can upload them to Facebook. The only limitation (besides Facebook's Code of Conduct) is that the video can be no longer than 20 minutes and no larger than 1024MB (one gigabyte).

Facebook supports numerous digital video formats, including Mobile Video (*.3g2, *.3gp, *.3gpp), Windows Media Video (*.asf and *.wmv), AVI Video (*.avi), Flash Video (*.flv), MPEG Video (*.mpeg, *.mpe, *.mpg, *.dat), MPEG-4 Video (*.m4v, *.mp4, *.mpeg4), Matroska Format (*.mkv), MOD Video (*.mod), QuickTime Movie (*.mov, *.qt), Nullsoft Video (*.nsv), Ogg Format (*.ogm, *.ogv), TOD (*.tod), and DVD Video (*.vob).

To upload a digital video file from your computer, take the following steps:

1. Head to your Profile and click the **Video** tab.

2. Click **+ Upload** (upper right). The Create a New Video page appears.

3. Click **Browse.** The Choose File to Upload dialog box appears.

4. Navigate to the folder where the digital video file is stored and select the file. As soon as you select the file, Facebook starts uploading it and displays a form you can fill out while you're waiting.

5. Enter any information you want to include with the video, including a title, description, and privacy settings to determine who can and can't view the video.

6. Click **Save Information.**

For instructions on how to upload videos from your cell phone or other mobile device, see Chapter 15.

Recording Video Using Your Webcam

If you're in the mood to make and post a spur-of-the-moment video, plug a webcam into your computer, and you instantly convert it into a digital video recorder. With the addition of Facebook, you can now film yourself on the fly and instantly upload the clip to Facebook. Here's what you do:

1. Head to your Profile and click the **Video** tab.

2. Click **Record** (upper right).

3. If the Camera box appears, use it to select the type of webcam you're using and then click the **Close** button.

4. If Facebook prompts you to allow it access to your camera and microphone, click **Allow.** The Create a New Video page appears, prompting you to start recording.

5. Click **Record** and then proceed to ham it up in front of the camera. (After you click Record, the button changes into a Stop button.)

6. When you're done with the show, click **Stop.**

7. Click **Play** to view the video.

8. Take one of the following steps:

   • If you don't like the clip, click **Reset** and head back to Step 5 for a reshoot.

   • If you like the clip, click **Save.** This takes you to the Edit Video page, where you can enter information about the video.

9. Enter any information you want to include with the video, including a title, description, and privacy settings to determine who can and can't view the video. You can also choose a frame of the video to serve as the thumbnail that represents it.

10. Click **Save.** Facebook saves your video and posts it to your Wall and News Feed to share with friends.

FRIEND-LY ADVICE

When recording, try to look at the camera rather than the screen. Otherwise, you appear to be looking away from your audience.

Click Record to start

Film yourself live!

Editing Video Information

After you upload or record a video, you can edit any information you entered and make other changes, such as rotating the clip 90 degrees clockwise or counterclockwise (if you shot it at an angle).

To edit the video, click **Profile** (in the top menu), click your **Video** tab, and then click the video you want to edit. This displays the video on its own page, where you can select any of the following options:

- **Share:** Post the video to your Wall and News Feed, or send it as a message attachment to your Facebook friends.

- **Rotate Left:** Rotate the video counterclockwise 90 degrees.

- **Rotate Right:** Rotate the video clockwise 90 degrees.

- **Tag This Video:** Tag yourself or a friend in the video.

- **Edit This Video:** Modify the title, description, or privacy settings associated with the video. You can also tag yourself or your friends in the video and choose a different frame to use as the video's thumbnail.

- **Delete Video:** Remove the video from your Facebook account, which removes it from your Wall and News Feed, too.

- **Embed This Video:** Obtain a code you can add to web pages or blog posts that displays a box in which the video plays. The following section provides additional details about embedding a video.

Embedding a Video

If you have your own web page or blog, you can embed your Facebook videos on your web pages or include them in your blog posts. Here's what you do:

1. Click **Profile** (in the top menu), click your **Videos** tab, and click the video you want to edit.

2. Click **Embed This Video**. The Embed Your Video box appears.

3. Click in the **Embed code** text box to highlight the code and then press **Ctrl+C** (on a PC) or **Command+C** (on a Mac), to copy it.

4. Open the web page or blog post in which you want to embed the video, and make sure you're editing the page or post in HTML view.

5. Click where you want to embed the video.

6. Press **Ctrl+V** (on a PC) or **Command+V** (on a Mac) to insert the embed code.

7. Save your web page or blog post.

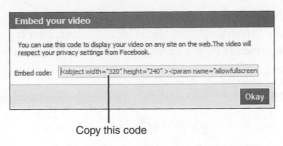

Copy this code

You can embed a Facebook video on a web page or blog post.

Whenever someone views your web page or blog post, a small box appears with a Play button inside it that the visitor can click to play the video. The cool thing is that, because the video is stored on Facebook and not on your web-hosting service, none of your resources are required to play the video—in other words, you're not using up any of your storage space or bandwidth.

Sending a Video Message via E-Mail

Tired of sending plain text messages? Add some spark with a video clip. On Facebook, it's easy—especially if you already uploaded or recorded a clip. To send a video that's already on Facebook (your own video or a Facebook friend's), here's what you do:

1. Display the video on its own page. For example, head to your Profile, click your **Video** tab, and then click one of your videos, or you can click a video in your News Feed and then click its title (below the video).

2. Click **Share** (to the right of the video). The Post to Profile box opens.

3. Click **Send as a Message Instead.** The Send as a Message box appears.

4. Click in the **To** box and type the names of one or more Facebook friends.

5. Click in the **Message** box and type a message to accompany the video. It's always a good idea to let people know why they might like to watch it.

6. Click **Send Message.**

You can send a video clip as a message attachment to your Facebook friends.

The Least You Need to Know

- Videos on Facebook cannot contain content that is hateful, threatening, or pornographic, or that contains nudity or graphic or gratuitous violence. In addition, any video you post must be shot by you or a Facebook friend and contain you or at least one of your Facebook friends.

- To access your Videos, click **Profile** and then click your **Video** tab. Or, from your Home page, click **Photos** (in the left menu) and then **Video.**

- In the upper right of your Videos page, you'll see options for uploading or recording video.

- To comment on a video, click in the **Write a comment** box, type your comment, and press **Enter.**

- The Share option next to a video enables you to post the video to your News Feed or send it as a message attachment to your friends.

Getting Organized with Groups

In This Chapter

- Exploring group dynamics on Facebook
- Joining and leaving groups
- Mixing it up in group discussions
- Sharing photos, videos, and other cool stuff
- Launching your own group and gathering members

You and your friends on Facebook form a tightly knit clique, but Facebook also allows you to wander off and mingle with friends and others in *Groups*. Groups are useful for gathering former classmates; sharing information among family members; meeting people who share similar goals, values, or interests; facilitating communication among members of an organization; and so on. And you don't even have to be friends to do it.

In this chapter, we show you how to join a group, form your own groups, engage in discussions, and share stuff with your fellow group members.

A Group Is a Group Is a Group ...

Facebook groups are like gatherings around the water cooler, where you can wander away from your News Feed and Wall to enter discussions and share with friends and nonfriends alike in a more theme-oriented environment. On Facebook, you can create or join three types of groups.

- **Open:** Open groups allow Facebook members—friends and nonfriends alike—to share common interests and passions. They're great for promoting a political candidate, organizing a movement, or even networking with people in a particular field.

- **Closed:** Exclusive areas where only selected Facebook friends hang out. For example, you can create a group for the South Vernon High School class of 1998 and allow only members of that class to join.

- **Secret:** Super-secret, invitation-only clubs that don't even show up in Facebook search results. Secret groups are great for when you don't want outsiders on Facebook knowing what you're up to.

> **FRIEND-LY ADVICE**
>
> If you're working on a project with others, you can create a secret work group where members can discuss ideas, collaborate on solving problems, monitor progress, and schedule meetings.

Exploring Existing Groups

The first encounter most Facebook members have with groups is when they receive an invitation from a friend to join a group. (More information about responding to such invitations is provided later in this chapter.) However, you don't need to wait for an invitation to get involved in group activities. You can be more proactive by browsing groups or searching for groups that interest you.

Touring Your Groups Page

Before you head out to search for groups you may want to join, check out your Groups page. To get there from your Home page, click **Groups** in the left menu. The Groups page appears.

Invitations you received   You can create a new group

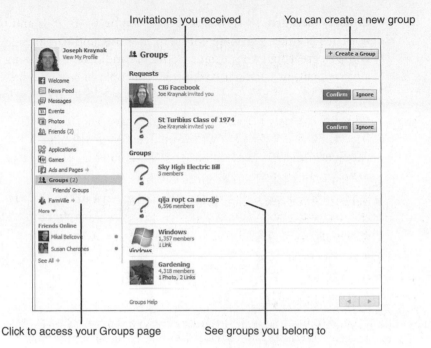

Click to access your Groups page   See groups you belong to

Get to know your Groups page.

POKE

Secret groups don't show up in the search results. Open groups have a Join Group link next to them. Closed groups have a Request to Join link next to them—you have to send a request to the group's administrator for admittance.

Searching for a Group

If you'd like to check out groups that focus on a specific interest or topic, search for groups by keyword or phrase:

1. Click in the **Search** box (in the top menu), type a keyword or two or three, and then click the **Search** button (the one with the magnifying glass on it) or press **Enter.** Facebook displays the top items that match your search entry. The search results may include people, groups, pages, posts by friends, and other items.

2. Click **Groups** (in the left menu).

3. To limit the list to certain categories click **Show: All Group Types** and click a category.

4. To limit the list even further, click **Show: All Subtypes** and click a subcategory.

5. Scroll down the list to browse available groups that match your search criteria.

6. When you reach the bottom of the list, you can click the right arrow button to view the next 10 groups in the list. (If you move forward, you can always move back by clicking the left-pointing triangle.)

Finding Groups Through Your Friends

Chances are good that if one of your close Facebook friends joins a group, it's worth checking out. Friends can turn you on to groups in several ways:

- **Invitation:** A friend can send you an invitation to join the group. Click **Confirm,** and you're in.

- **Your News Feed:** Whenever a friend joins a group, that activity may show up in your News Feed with a link to the group, unless your friend chose to remove that item from his Recent Activity area after joining the group. Click the link to head to the group's Home page.

- **Friends' Walls:** Whenever someone joins a group, the activity is posted on the person's Wall under Recent Activities. By pulling up a friend's profile and checking her Wall, you can check out which groups your friend has recently joined.

To find out how to prevent the Groups app from posting updates to your News Feed or hide the fact that you joined a particular group, skip ahead to the section "Joining a Group."

Checking Out a Group

After you've found a few groups that possibly match your interests, you can inspect them more closely. Click the group's name or the picture that represents it, and the group's Home page pops up.

An open group's Home page lets you sample the group before joining it.

A closed group's Home page severely restricts access for nonmembers. You may see some basic information, but you probably won't see the Wall, Discussion Board, or member list until you join.

Getting Involved in a Group

To get involved in a group and share with its members, you must first join the group. As you'll see in the following sections, joining and leaving a group are two of the easiest things you can do on Facebook.

Joining a Group

All you need to do to join an open group on Facebook is click the **Join Group** link and then click the **Join** button when prompted to confirm, and you gain instant access. To join a closed group, click the **Request to Join** link. You then have to wait for the administrator to confirm your request. You don't have to keep checking; when you're allowed in, you receive a notification letting you know. If your request is denied or ignored, you don't receive notification.

To keep your membership status in groups more private, adjust your Groups application settings. Click **Account** (top menu) and then **Application Settings.** Next to Groups, click **Edit Settings.** You can change your Profile settings to have the Groups tab or box on your profile visible only to friends or friends of friends. To hide it altogether, open the **Privacy** menu, click **Customize,** open the **These people** menu, click **Only Me,** and click **Save Setting.** To prevent Groups from publishing to your Profile or News Feed, click the **Additional Permissions** tab and remove the checkmark from **Publish content to my Wall.**

Leaving a Group

If you happen to lose interest in a group, you can leave at any time. Click the **Groups** icon (in the left menu). Click the name or photo of the group you want to leave, click **Leave Group** (last option below group picture on left), and click **Remove** when prompted to confirm. That's it. You're outta there.

Conversing in Groups

Groups provide two means of communication, each of which has a distinct purpose. Before you post anything to the group, choose the best place to post:

- **The Wall:** A group Wall is like your Wall—a place where group members can post information listed in reverse chronological order (most recent first).

- **Discussion Board:** On a Discussion Board, group members can create discussion topics that other members can then contribute to. As long as members stay on point, group discussions proceed in a fairly orderly fashion, making discussions easier to follow.

In the following sections, we show you how to post updates to your group's Wall and carry on discussions via the Discussion Board.

WHOA!

Group administrators have a tremendous amount of control over the features available in a group. They can prevent nonadministrators from posting to the group Wall; choose not to allow photos, video, or links to be posted; and even completely disable the discussion board. Don't be surprised if you're unable to do some (or all) of what we describe in the following sections.

Posting Status Updates to the Group Wall

As long as you're comfortable reading and posting updates on your Wall or News Feed, you can smoothly transition to the group Wall.

When you're ready to post a message to the group, click in the **Write something ...** box, type your message, and click **Share.**

Share with the group via the group Wall.

Carrying on Group Discussions

When you're ready to carry on a conversation with your fellow group members, you have two choices—join in a discussion already in progress, or initiate your own discussion.

> **NETIQUETTE**
>
> Starting a new discussion on the same topic is poor manners. Prior to initiating a discussion, check whether a discussion on the same topic is already in progress. Head to the group's Home page and click the Discussions tab to view a list of topics under discussion. If more than 30 topics are under discussion, Facebook doesn't display all of them. In such a case, you can click **See All Topics** just above the list of topics to check out the entire list.

Jump into a discussion at any time by clicking the link for the desired topic. This displays the Topic View for the selected topic. To post a reply, click **Reply to Topic,** click in the **Reply** box, type your message, and click **Post reply.**

If nobody in the group has launched a topic you'd like to see the group discuss, consider starting a new topic. Click **Start New Topic** to view the Start New Topic page. Click in the **Topic** box, type a topic name, click in the **Post** box, type a message to initiate the discussion, and click **Post new topic.** Facebook displays the new discussion, starting with your initial message.

Type a topic name

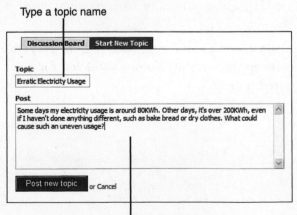

Type a message to get things rolling

Start a new topic.

Sharing Photos, Links, and Events with a Group

Unless the group's administrator has prohibited members from posting photos or video clips or announcing events, you should see a separate tab for each. Each tab enables group members to post a specific type of content on a page, to keep it from getting lost amid the clutter of Wall posts. To share a photo or video with the group or announce an upcoming event, start by clicking the appropriate tab:

- **Photo:** On the Photos page, click **+ Add Group Photos.** The Add from My Photos page appears. You can then add photos stored in one of your Facebook photo albums or click the **Upload Photos** tab to upload new photos stored on your computer. (The Edit Photos tab lets you edit or delete photos you're already sharing with the group.) For more about working with photos, see Chapter 7.

- **Video:** On the Video page, click **+ Upload** to upload a video file from your computer to the group's video page or click **Record** to record a new video using a webcam attached to your computer. For more about working with videos, see Chapter 8.

- **Events:** On the Events page, click **+ Create Event,** and then follow the onscreen instructions to enter details about the event and send out invitations to group members. See Chapter 11 for more about announcing events.

As photos, links, video clips, and events are posted, a separate box for each type of item appears in the column on the left for quick access to recently posted content.

Edit photos you're sharing with the group

Upload new photos

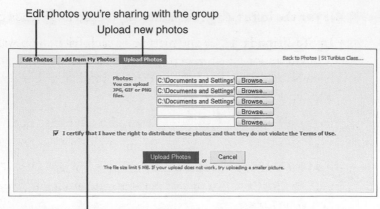

Add photos from an existing photo album

You can share your photos with the group.

Creating Your Own Group

If you think all the existing groups on Facebook are lame-o, create your own group. It's easy:

1. From your Home page, click the **Groups** icon (in the left menu).

2. Click **+ Create a Group.** The Create a Group page appears displaying the Step 1: Group Info form.

3. Complete the form, entering a name for the group, a brief description, and the group type and subtype. (Optionally, you can enter recent news and contact information.)

4. Click **Create Group.** Facebook creates the group and displays the Step 2: Customize form.

5. Enter your group settings to control which features the group supports (events, discussion board, photos, video, and so on) and choose an access type (open, closed, or secret).

6. Click **Save.** Facebook saves your settings and displays a page that enables you to invite your friends and others to join the group.

7. Enter the information requested on the Invite Friends page:

• **Invite Friends:** Click the picture of each friend you want to invite to join your group. (To narrow the collection of friends displayed, click in the **Find Friends** text box, and start typing a friend's name.)

• **Invite People via E-Mail:** Use this box to invite non-Facebook members, via their e-mail addresses, to join you.

• **Add a Personal Message:** Click in this box and type a message to accompany your invitation to encourage invitees to join your group.

8. Click **Send Invitations.** Your invitations are sent, and you return to the Invite Friends page.

When you're done creating the group, head to the group's Home page, mouse over the Profile photo placeholder, click **Change Picture,** and then upload a photo or snap a photo using your webcam. It's always nice to have a photo for your group.

From the group's Home page, you can change the group's settings by clicking **Edit Group Settings** (just below the group's Profile photo). To change information you entered about the group, click the **Info** tab, click **Edit Information** (upper right), and edit the information as desired.

Enter your official website address (if any)

Upload a picture

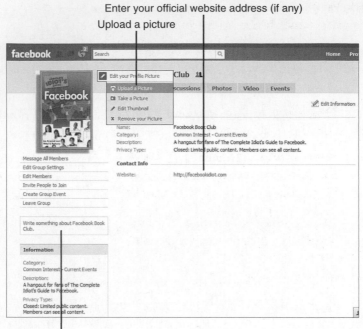

Write a brief description of your group

Enter your Group settings.

Managing Your Group

Creating a group is only half the fun. As people join your group, you must attend to your duties as group administrator. Your most important duty is to monitor Wall posts and discussions. As people post messages, read through them to identify any messages that are inappropriate.

On the Wall, you can click **Report** to report any posts that fail to comply with Facebook's terms of service or you feel are worthy of turning over to the Facebook police. If you just don't want the message on the group Wall, mouse over it and click **Remove.**

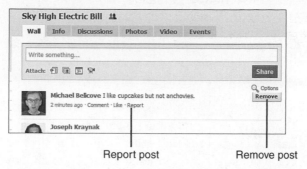

Report post   Remove post

Monitor Wall posts and discussions for irrelevant and inappropriate content.

In a discussion, you can use the following links next to each message to remove or report it:

- **Mark as Irrelevant:** Click **Mark as Irrelevant** to hide the post from the group without deleting it. This is helpful if you feel the person posting the message failed to include an important piece of information and you want to talk with them about it before the entire group reads and reacts to the post.

- **Report:** Let Facebook know that someone in your group is posting inappropriate content. (You may want to warn the person first, by replying to her directly and giving her a chance to mend her ways. You can also remove or block the person from the group as explained later.)

- **Delete Post:** Remove the message from the discussion.

Next to the content *you* post in a discussion are two links: **Edit Post** and **Delete Post.** If you post on the Wall, you can't edit the post, but you can delete it.

Your group's Home page allows you to perform additional administrative duties. To begin, click **Groups** in the left menu, and then click the name of the group you want to manage. The group's Home page appears. Off to the left are links that allow you to perform the following duties as group administrator.

- **Message All Members:** Send a message to all group members.

- **Edit Group Settings:** Change the group preferences (including what appears on the group's Home page and what members are allowed to upload).

- **Edit Members:** The Edit Members screen is particularly useful for removing members from the group, blocking their readmittance, and making other group members administrators, so you don't have to manage the group all by yourself.

- **Invite People to Join:** Click this link to send out more invitations to join the group.

- **Create Group Event:** Schedule an Event and announce it to the group. For more about events, check out Chapter 11.

- **Leave Group:** You can leave the group at any time, but if you choose to leave, you may want to name an administrator to replace you prior to your departure. If you're the only administrator, and you leave, Facebook offers the position to other group members. If you're the only remaining member of the group and you leave, the group is dissolved.

Group administration links

You can perform various administrative duties for the group.

The Least You Need to Know

- Groups allow you to mingle with Facebook friends and others and engage in discussions outside the more public venues of Walls and News Feeds.

- To head to your Groups page, click **Groups** in the left menu.

- You can find groups by performing a search with the Search box in the top menu, receiving an invitation to join, seeing in your News Feed that a friend joined a particular group, or pulling up a friend's Profile to see the groups she's joined listed under her Recent Activities.

- The Discussion Board is better than the Wall at keeping discussions on topic.

- To create your own group, go to your Groups page, click **+ Create a Group,** and follow the on-screen instructions.

Chatting with Friends in Real Time

In This Chapter

- Chatting with friends using Facebook's instant-messaging tool
- Starting and ending a chat session
- Hiding from friends when you're not to be bothered
- Customizing chat

When friends are online, you may have the opportunity to carry on a conversation with them using Facebook's chat application. If you're familiar with AOL Instant Messenger, Yahoo! Instant Messenger, or any of the many other instant-messaging programs out there, you know the drill—you select the person you want to chat with from your list of friends, click the **Chat** button, and start typing. As you chat, whatever you type appears on her screen, and whatever she types appears on yours. (If you're not familiar with instant messaging, don't worry—it's easier than e-mail, and we step you through the process.)

In this chapter, you discover how to initiate and navigate a typical Facebook Chat session, set your chat options, and use friend lists to more effectively track the people you're chatting with.

Let's Chat!

Compared to other chat programs, Facebook Chat is the stripped down, no-frills model. Assuming one of your friends is logged in and online (more about the online thing in a minute), initiating a chat session is a breeze:

1. Click **Chat** (in the lower-right corner of any Facebook screen). A menu appears listing the names of any friends who are online.

2. Click the name of the friend you want to engage in a chat session. This displays a chat box.

3. Type a message and press **Enter** on your keyboard. Your message pops up in the chat box. Assuming your friend responds, his message pops up right below yours.

Click here to end the chat session

Type a message   Click Chat
and press Enter

Chat on Facebook with your friends.

You can carry on chat sessions with more than one friend at a time. Each chat session appears in its own box with its own tab. To change from one chat session to another, click the tab for the friend you want to chat with.

You can click the Minimize button (the dash) in the upper-right corner of any chat window to make the window disappear without closing it. A tab for the window appears (typically the bottom right of the screen), and a balloon icon appears to notify you whenever someone sends you a chat message. If your speakers are on and the volume's turned up, you'll also hear an audio cue whenever someone sends you a new message—and if you look closely, the title of your browser window, which normally reads "Facebook | <page you're on>," flashes "New Message from …!" when a new chat message first appears on screen.

When you're ready to end a session, just click the **X** next to your friend's name.

If one of your friends sends you a message to start a chat session, a chat box pops up, allowing you to reply.

That's it. Short chapter, huh? Well, not exactly. Chat includes some additional features, and we'll spend the rest of the chapter exploring those.

POKE

On Facebook, you can chat only with friends, not strangers. To contact someone who's not your friend, head to the person's Profile and click the link to send them a message. For more about sending messages, see Chapter 5. For details on friending someone, see Chapter 3.

Viewing and Deleting Your Chat History

Facebook keeps a short log of your chat history so you can pick up where you left off when you ended your last chat session with a friend. When you begin a new chat session, you can see the last few lines of your previous session.

You can clear the chat history at any time to prevent snoopy family members or officemates from nosing in on your business or just reduce the clutter of messages. Just above the area where the chat discussion is displayed, click **Clear Chat History.**

Clear your chat history

The chat history lets you and your friend pick up where you left off.

Going Offline or Back Online

Unless you tell Facebook otherwise, whenever you're logged in, you're online and ready to chat. If a friend opens his Chat menu, your name appears on that menu, and he can click it to start chatting with you. If you choose to go offline, you're invisible and friends can't tell you're online and can't bug you. To go offline or come back online, here's what you do:

- **Go offline:** Click **Chat, Options, Go Offline.**

- **Go online:** Click **Chat.**

POKE

When you're offline, a gray dot appears next to Chat in your Chat bar, your status is shown as (Offline), and your name does not appear on your friends' Chat menus. When you or your friends are online and are chatting, a solid green dot appears next to your name. When you or your friends are logged on but inactive (haven't done anything on Facebook for at least 10 minutes), a green quarter-moon icon appears next to your names.

You can make yourself available to specific friends or friend lists exclusively (and hide from others). More information on these options can be found near the end of this chapter.

Click Chat, Options, Go Offline to hide

Click Chat to go online

You can go offline to be incommunicado.

Setting Your Chat Options

Although Facebook Chat is slim and trim, it does offer a few optional accessories, including a larger, pop out chat window and audio cues. In the following sections, we show you how to access these accessories.

Pop Out Chat

Those teeny-tiny chat boxes are nice for exchanging a few short pleasantries with your Facebook friends, but if you're engaged in a deep conversation or are chatting with multiple friends, they can be very difficult to manage. Fortunately, Facebook enables you to trade in those chat boxes for a full-size chat window devoted solely to talking amongst your friends.

To display the chat window, click **Chat, Options, Pop out Chat.** The chat window appears. To change from one chat session to another, click the tab for the friend you want to chat with.

You can close the window by clicking the **X** in the upper-right corner. This doesn't end your chat sessions; it just returns you to the chat boxes that appear at the bottom of the Facebook screen. You can also return to pop in chat by clicking **Options, Pop in Chat.**

Pop out chat gives you a dedicated window in which to converse.

Play Sound for New Messages

Assuming you have speakers or earphones plugged into your computer and they're turned on, whenever someone sends you a message, Facebook dings you. Actually it sounds more like the popping noise you make when you smack your lips. You can toggle this option on or off—click **Chat, Options, Play Sound for New Messages.**

Keep Online Friends Window Open

When you click Chat, the menu that pops up is actually referred to as the *Online Friends Window*. If you click to do something else on Facebook, like heading back to your Home page, the window disappears. If you'd like the Online Friends Window to remain open as you cruise around Facebook, click **Chat, Options, Keep Online Friends Window Open.** (If you choose Options from the Online Friends Window, the menu may not contain this option. Try clicking **Chat** [lower-right corner of the main Facebook screen], and then **Options, Keep Online Friends Window Open.**)

Check Keep Online Friends Window Open

You can keep the Online Friends Window open while you wander Facebook.

Show Only Names in Online Friends

Unless you specify otherwise, Facebook displays the names and Profile photos of your friends in the Online Friends Window. You can omit the photos to make room for displaying more names. Click **Chat, Options, Show Only Names in Online Friends.**

Setting Friend List Options

With friend lists, described in Chapter 3, you can keep lists of friends separate. This can come in very handy when you're chatting online. You can display friends by lists, go offline with one list while remaining online with another, or even choose to engage in an intimate discussion with your BFF without the distractions from other friends who may want to strike up a conversation.

Display or Hide a Friend List

When numerous friends are online chatting, the Online Friends Window can get awfully cluttered. One way to reduce the clutter and more effectively manage chat sessions is to group your friends by friend list.

To turn a friend list on or off, click **Chat, Friend List,** and click the list you want to display or hide. A checkmark indicates the friend list is displayed.

Click a friend list

You can group online chatters by friend list.

When you choose a friend list, any friends on the selected list are moved from the full list of online friends to the section representing the selected friend list.

Go Offline or Online with a Group of Friends

When you have chatters grouped by friend lists, you can go offline with one or more groups of friends while remaining online with others. Rest the mouse pointer on the icon to the right of the friend list you want to be offline with and when you see Go Offline, click the icon.

POKE

When a friend on one of your friend lists becomes inactive, his name completely disappears from the friend list in the Online Friends Window instead of just having the quarter-moon icon appear next to his name.

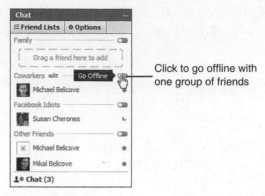

You can go offline with one group of friends and remain online with others.

Create a New Friend List

You can create a friend list on the fly. Click **Chat, Friend Lists,** and then click in the **Create a new list box.** Type a name for the new list, and press **Enter.** The new list appears. You can now drag friends from the Online Friends Window into the designated area to add them to your friend list.

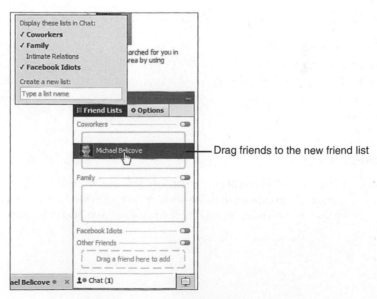

You can create a new friend list on the fly.

POKE

Facebook Chat is supported by a number of non-Facebook instant-messaging clients, including Adium, Digsby, eBuddy, faceoffIM, Flock, Nimbuzz, and Scrapboy, all of which enable you to chat with your friends even if you're not logged in to Facebook.

The Least You Need to Know

- To strike up a conversation with a friend who's currently online, click **Chat** and then click the friend's name.
- To go offline and hide from friends who may want to chat with you, click **Chat, Options, Go Offline.**
- To go back online, click **Chat.**
- To display a dedicated chat window, click **Chat, Options, Pop out Chat.**
- You can arrange names in the Online Friends Window by list. Click **Chat, Friend Settings,** and then the desired friend list.

Partay! Tracking and Announcing Events

In This Chapter

- Meeting your own personal events planner
- Finding out what's happening
- Responding to an invitation
- Planning your own event and announcing it

Party at Mikal's house, Saturday night, 6 pm till ?:?? am, BYOB! Food, ice, and entertainment provided! Be sure to RSVP, so we know how much pizza to order!

Yep, announcing an event on Facebook is as easy and inexpensive as that. No mailing invitations. No phone calls and answering machines. All you do is compose your event announcement, set your preferences, choose the friends you want to invite, and wait for them to RSVP or just show up. Whether you're planning a small get-together or a major public gathering like a benefit, concert, or grand opening, Facebook's Events application has everything you need to spread the word, take a head count of likely attendees, and keep everyone in the loop regarding any change of plans.

If you're planning an upcoming event, this chapter can play a key role in your event planning. If you're just looking for something to do, you'll discover how to tune in to announcements of upcoming events and respond to any invitations you happen to receive.

Accessing and Navigating the Events Application

Whenever you're planning an event or in the mood for some action, head to the Events application. To get there from your Home page, click **Events** (the calendar-looking thingy in the left menu). The Events page appears, supplying you with a list of events along with a button for creating a new event. Consider this page your launch pad for doing everything else explained in this chapter.

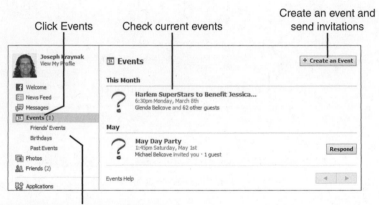

Click Events Check current events Create an event and send invitations

Check friends' events and birthdays

The Events application lets you check upcoming events and plan new events.

Checking Scheduled Events

Why deal with the hassle of planning an event when you can just show up at someone else's shindig, trash his space, eat his food, and head home for a much-needed nap? With Facebook's Events application, you have access to your own party line 24/7. You can check out events your friends have in the works, poke around for events that might grab your attention, or search for specific events by school, location, favorite bands, favorite comedians, or anything else that twists your imagination. The following sections show you how.

Poking Around for Events

The quickest way to keep tabs on upcoming events, friends' events, past events, and birthdays is to use the options that appear below Events after you click it. Click **Friends' Events,** for example, and you can check out all the events your Facebook friends are planning to attend or are hosting.

Get more information

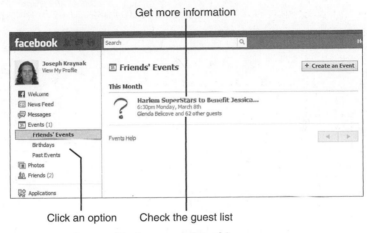

Click an option   Check the guest list

Check out your friends' events.

Click the event's title to find out more about it, including more about the date, time, and location; a full description of the event; a list of confirmed guests as well as people who've said they're not coming or may be coming and people who haven't yet responded to their invitations; any comments guests have chosen to post on the event's Wall; and links you can use to contact the administrators (the hosts or admins).

Under **Your RSVP,** you can let the hosts know whether you're attending, may be attending, or will not be attending the event. (More details about RSVP-ing are provided later in this chapter.) You can also click the **Share** option to e-mail the event to your friends or post it to your Profile.

FRIEND-LY ADVICE

Use the **Export** option to send the event to another application, such as iCal for the iPhone, so you can carry the event with you when you're not sitting at your computer. For more about using Facebook with a mobile device, check out Chapter 15.

Who, when, and where   RSVP

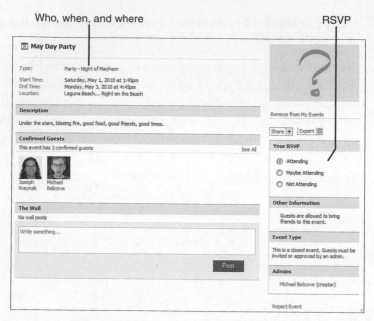

When you click an event, you get the full scoop.

Searching and Browsing Events

Bored? Nothing to do on a Friday night? Wrong! There's plenty
going on. You just don't know about it. Now with Facebook, you can
search for and browse events near or far to find potentially engaging
activities.

Perhaps the best way to search for an event is to head to your Home
page, click **Events,** and then use the Events page to check out what
all your friends are doing.

To expand your horizons beyond what your Facebook friends are up
to, you can search for events by type of event, the name of a band
or comedian, a school name, location (city or town), special interest
(like volleyball), and so on. Here's what you do to search for events:

1. Click in the **Search** box (top menu), type one or two words
    describing the sort of event you're interested in (for example,
    "comedy chicago"), and press **Enter.** Facebook displays
    events, groups, pages, and other stuff that matches your
    search instructions.

2. Click **Events** (in the left menu). Facebook narrows the list to show only events.

3. To narrow the list of events, select options from the **Show All Dates** or **All Event Types** lists. For example, you can narrow the list to show only events for the upcoming week or only sports events. If you choose a category, you can also choose a subcategory to narrow the list of events even more.

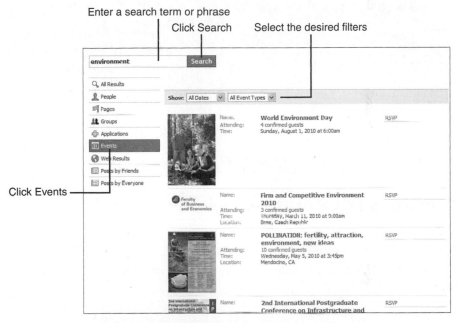

Perform a broad search and then narrow the results, if necessary.

RSVP-ing an Event You Plan to Attend

Whether you've been invited to an event or plan on crashing one, RSVP the hosts to let them know whether you're coming, not coming, or unsure. Besides being the polite thing to do, your RSVP serves several practical purposes. For one, it helps the hosts take a head count, so they can prepare for the hungry, thirsty hordes due to arrive at the event.

Perhaps more importantly, your RSVP (especially if you're planning to attend) spreads the word about the event. Your RSVP is status-update worthy, and it shows up in your News Feed, on your Wall, and in some cases—if you edit your Event preferences to allow for this—on all your friends' News Feeds. You also show up in the event's Confirmed Guests list and, as everyone knows, a crowd usually draws a crowd.

By RSVP-ing, you get a perk, too. If the hosts change plans or cancel the event and are responsible enough to make those changes on Facebook, you receive a notification on Facebook and via e-mail (assuming you didn't disable e-mail notifications for Events).

RSVP-ing is a snap. Just head to the event's page and under **Your RSVP,** click **Attending, Maybe Attending,** or **Not Attending.** If you received a personal invitation via e-mail, you can use the same options to inform your hosts.

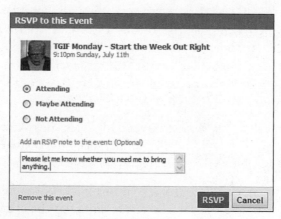

Be polite by RSVP-ing to the hosts.

Announcing Your Own Special Event

Whether you're planning a family get-together, a slam poetry competition, or a political rally, you need to get the word out to your people. The easiest way to is to create an event listing on Facebook. All you do is specify the who, what, when, where, and why and select the friends you want to invite. Facebook does the rest, sending out all your invitations in the blink of an eye. If plans change, just edit the event, and Facebook notifies everyone on your guest list!

In the following sections, we show you how to create and customize an event, invite guests, take a head count, print a guest list, and more. And in the unfortunate circumstance that your event fizzles, we even show you how to cancel it.

NETIQUETTE

Be polite. If you're invited to an event, RSVP. Don't invite people you don't really know to a highly personal event, like a birthday party or baby shower. And if you're coordinating an event, don't overpromote it or send too many reminders to your friends.

Creating an Event

Creating an event certainly sounds easy enough, but if this is your first time, you may be surprised at the amount of information to enter and the number of options to check. Perhaps the biggest challenge is entering everything correctly. One small slip and you could end up announcing that surprise birthday party to the entire Facebook community. Wouldn't that be a surprise?!

Creating an event is a three-step process: enter the essential information, customize the event to enter preferences and control access to it, and then send invitations to the prospective attendees.

Start the process of creating an event using one of the following methods, depending on whether you're planning the event for your Facebook friends or for a Facebook group you administer:

- **Event for Friends:** From your Home page, click **Events** (in the left menu). Click **+ Create an Event.** The Create an Event page appears, prompting you to begin the three-step process.

- **Group Event:** Pull up the group's page, as explained in Chapter 9, and then click **Create Group Event** (left menu). By creating the event from the group's page, you'll have the option, in Step 3 of the process, to invite all group members simply by clicking a checkbox.

In Step 1, all you have to enter is an event tagline (a name for the event), but you should also enter the event's location and a starting and ending date and time. Be sure to set the privacy level for this event; by default, all invitees are allowed to invite others. You can choose to Close the event so invitees can RSVP but not invite others or make the event Secret so only invitees can see information about the event. When you're done entering information for Step 1, click **Create Event** to create the event and forge ahead to Step 2.

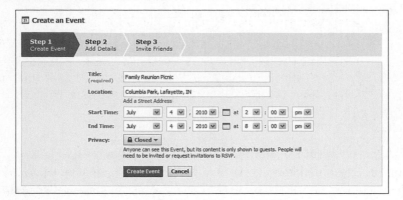

Enter details about the event.

WHOA!

Think twice about entering contact information in your event description. People can contact you through Facebook. You don't need to risk having your e-mail address or phone number fall into the wrong hands.

Nothing in Step 2 is required, but we recommend that you upload a picture and type a description, so everyone you invite will know what the party's all about. Above the Description box, you can also choose an event category and type. (If you choose a category, choose a type, too.) The most important options are near the bottom of this screen, under Event Options:

- **Enable the event wall:** To encourage some preparty chatter about the event, leave the event's Wall enabled. If you're concerned that people will post inappropriate or inane updates, click the option to disable the Wall.

- **Enable the event photos, videos, and links:** If you're concerned about people posting inappropriate photos, video, or links, you can click this option to prevent anyone from posting this type of content, or leave this option checked and select **Only allow admins to post content to the event** to allow only administrators to post photos, videos, and links.

- **Allow guests to bring friends to the event:** By default, invitees are allowed to bring guests. To let them know they must leave their significant others behind, uncheck this option.

- **Show the guest list:** By default, Facebook displays the guest list, so invitees can see who's attending before they accept or refuse the invitation. Depending on the nature of the party, people may not want others to know whether they will be in attendance. You can uncheck this option to keep the guest list hidden.

When you're done with Step 2, click **Save and Continue.** Unless you're creating a secret event, a dialog box pops up asking whether you want to publish the event to your Wall and your friend's Home pages. Click **Publish** or **Skip** (to not publish the event) and proceed to Step 3, in which you choose friends to invite.

In Step 3, all you do is click on the name or photo of the friends you want to invite. If you're creating an event for a Facebook group you administer, Step 3 includes a checkbox near the bottom labeled **Invite members of the host group,** which you can click to send invitations to all group members. To invite non-Facebook members click in the **Invite People via Email** box and type the e-mail addresses of the people you want to invite, separating addresses with a comma. You can also choose to import e-mail addresses from Outlook or a web-based e-mail address book. (For more about importing e-mail addresses, see Chapter 3.)

After you've specified all the people you want to invite, click in the **Add a Personal Message** box, type a brief message, such as "Please join us for a private screening of *Zorg and Andy*, a comedy about love, duty, and sacrifice ... human sacrifice." Check your message, make sure you selected all the friends you want to invite, and click **Send Invitations.** Instantly, your personal event planner delivers e-mail invitations to everyone on your list.

After sending out your invitations, Facebook displays the page for the event. Carefully inspect your event for any errors. If you see something that's not right, click **Edit Event,** enter your changes, and click **Save Changes.** (If you wandered off to do something else on Facebook, you can always pull up your event from your Home page by clicking **Events** in the left menu and clicking the event's tagline or by pulling up your Profile and clicking the **Events** tab.)

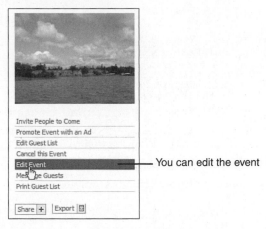

Your event is born.

Managing Your Event

After distributing the invitations, you can kick back and wait for the RSVPs to start rolling in. As they arrive, you may want to return to your event to perform your event administrator duties:

- **Invite People to Come:** More people, that is.

- **Edit Guest List:** See who's coming, who's not, and who may be; uninvite people by removing them from the list; or block people to prevent them from crashing your party (although you may need a doorman or bouncer on the day of the event to actually enforce it).

- **Cancel This Event:** If you get a bunch of no-shows or simply can't be there yourself, you can always cancel. Facebook notifies all invitees and lets you add a personal message to the notification.

- **Edit Event:** Change information about the event, including the date and time. You can also change the event settings.

- **Message Guests:** Send an e-mail message to all the people who've said they're coming or may be coming.

- **Print Guest List:** You can choose to print a list of all invitees; only those attending; those attending and maybe attending; or those attending, maybe attending, and not attending. You can also choose to have Profile photos included in whichever list you choose to print.

Manage your event.

If you need help planning or managing an event, consider adding an administrator. On the event's page, click **Edit Guest List** and then click **Make Admin** next to the person you want to promote to administrator.

The Least You Need to Know

- To fire up the Events application from your Home page, click the **Events** icon in the left menu.

- After you click Events, more options appear enabling you to view friends' events, birthdays, and past events.

- If you're invited to an event, be sure to RSVP. It's the polite thing to do and keeps you in the loop.

- Use the **Search** box in the top menu to search for events, and then click **Events** in the left menu to show only events in the search results.

- To announce your own event, click the **Events** icon (left menu), click the **+ Create an Event** button (upper right), and then follow the onscreen instructions.

Taking Notes ... and Sharing Them

Chapter

12

In This Chapter

- Grasping the basic concept of notes
- Reading and commenting on notes—yours, a friend's, a business's, or notes about you
- Posting and sharing notes
- Importing blog entries as notes
- Passing notes in private

After about 60 seconds on Facebook, you know what a status update is, but ask most members what a Facebook note is, and you'll probably get a blank stare—or the person will fudge and make up some answer like, "A note is more like a reminder to yourself."

Well, that's not quite right. A note is much more than that, as you'll see in this chapter.

What Are Notes Exactly?

Notes are Facebook's answer to blogging. If you're not all that sure what blogging is all about, think of it as journaling or keeping a diary, with two primary differences:

- **Blogging is public (usually).** When you post a blog entry, it appears online where anyone can look at it. Facebook's Notes feature can give you more privacy than a typical blog because, by default, only your Facebook friends are privy to what you post.

- **Blogging is interactive.** People can comment on your blog entries if you let them, and usually you want to let them because, well, that's sorta the point of blogging—you post something and it sparks discussion. Blogging is all about creating an open forum where people can freely exchange information, observations, insights, and opinions. In addition, the more activity your blog entries inspire, the more search engine traffic you attract.

In the world of Facebook, you use notes instead of status updates when you have more to say. In addition, while status updates are exclusively of the plain-text variety, you can format a note using HTML (hypertext markup language) tags, such as <bold> for bold, <i> for italics, and <u> for an underline. In other words, you can get a little fancier with your formatting.

If you already have a blog, don't worry about having to pull double duty. Near the end of this chapter, we show you how to set up an RSS feed on Facebook that automatically pulls entries from your existing blog into Facebook and displays your entries as notes. Pretty cool, eh?

Entering the Notes Zone

Notes is a Facebook application (or app for short), but it's one of the few standard apps, along with Photos and Video, included as a core component of Facebook. To access the Notes app, click **Notes** (in the left menu of the Home page). (You may need to click **More,** below the list of apps, to bring Notes into view.) The Notes page appears displaying recent note activity, if any—friends' notes, your own, and notes about you. This page also provides a button (upper right) for posting a note of your own.

Recent Notes activity   Write a new Note

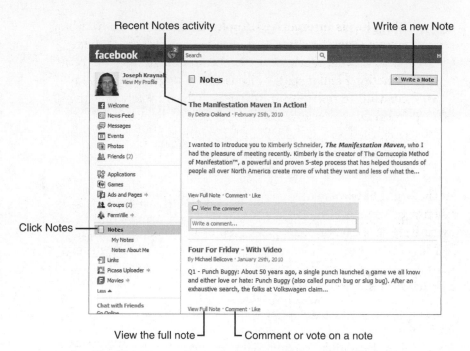

Click Notes

View the full note   Comment or vote on a note

The Notes page, where you can access all your Notes features.

Perusing Your Friends' Notes

The Notes page displays short notes or excerpts of longer notes your Facebook friends have recently posted. You can view a note on a page of its own by clicking the note's title or the **View Full Note** link above the comment box. To view all notes a friend has posted, click your friend's name to head to her Home page and then click the **Notes** tab.

On your friend's Notes tab, you can subscribe to your friend's notes. Under **Subscribe to these Notes** (to the right of the list of notes), click **...'s Notes** and then click **Subscribe to this feed.** This adds an entry to your browser's Feeds menu, giving you quick access to your friends' notes, regardless of whether you're logged on to Facebook.

Commenting on Existing Notes

When your friends post notes, they usually welcome comments. To post a comment, click in the **Write a comment** box below the note, type your comment, and click **Comment.** When you do, the friend who wrote the note and anyone else who already left a comment is notified, which sometimes results in even more comments.

Sharing Notes ... Or Not

Do you want to help your friend's note go viral? Then share it. You can share a note by posting it to your News Feed and Wall, where it shows up as a link, or you can share the link by sending a message to your Facebook friends.

To share your friend's note with all your friends via your News Feed and Wall, click the **Share** link, type a brief message explaining why you found the note worthy of sharing, and click **Share.**

To send the note to select friends via a message, click the **Share** link, click **Send as a message instead,** and then compose and send your message as explained in Chapter 5.

Posting a New Note

To post a note, pull up your Home page, click **Notes** (left menu), and click the **+ Write a Note** button. The Write a Note page appears. Click in the **Title** box and type a brief, descriptive, and compelling title for your note (otherwise, nobody will want to read it). Click in the **Body** box and type whatever you want to say. You can format the text by following the guide presented in Table 12.1.

POKE

HTML tags come in two flavors—paired and unpaired. For paired tags, you type a tag where you want the formatting to begin and another tag where you want it to end; for example <i>italics</i> displays *italics*. Unpaired codes stand alone, such as — which inserts an em dash that looks like this: —.

Table 12.1 HTML Tags for Formatting Notes

Format	HTML Tag
Bold	\Bold\
Italics	\<i>Italics\</i>
Underline	\<u>Underline\</u>
~~Strikethrough~~	\<s>Strikethrough\</s>
Big size	\<big>Big size\</big>
Small size	\<small>Small size\</small>
Em dash like —	\—
Hyperlink to FacebookIdiot.com	\<a href="http://facebookidiot.com">FacebookIdiot.com\</a>
Bulleted (unnumbered) list • Item • Item • Item • Item	\<ul> \<li>Item\</li> \<li>Item\</li> \<li>Item\</li> \<li>Item\</li> \</ul>
Numbered List 1. Step one 2. Step two 3. Step three 4. Step four	\<ol> \<li>Step one\</li> \<li>Step two\</li> \<li>Step three\</li> \<li>Step four\</li> \</ol>
Indented quote	\<blockquote>Indented quote\</blockquote>
Heading 1	\<h1>Heading 1\</h1>
Heading 2	\<h1>Heading 2\</h1>
Heading 3	\<h1>Heading 3\</h1>

After composing your note, you can tag Facebook friends mentioned in the note or friends whom you want to make sure know about the note. To tag a friend, click in the **Type any name** text box (upper-right corner of the Write a Note page), start typing your friend's name, and, when you see the name of the friend you want to tag, click it. Repeat the steps to tag other friends. After you post the note, Facebook automatically places a message on tagged friends' Walls about the existence of your note and sends them notifications (assuming they didn't disable notifications for notes).

You can write a note.

Below the Body box are options to **Upload a photo** (to attach a new photo to the note) or **Import a photo** to use a photo you already uploaded into one of your Facebook photo albums. No surprises here, but if you need a refresher course on working with photos in Facebook, head back to Chapter 7.

Below the **Import a photo** option, you'll find the **Note Privacy** settings. Open the **Note Privacy** list and select the option that best represents the Facebook members you want to be able to access your note: **Everyone, Friends of Friends, Only Friends,** or **Customize.** The Customize option enables you to make the note visible to **Only Me** or cherry-pick individuals who can see the note; for example, you can click **Specific People** and choose specific individuals or a friend list.

Reviewing Your Notes

Assuming this is your first encounter with the Notes app, you don't have any notes to review—but since you're on the notes page, let's talk about reviewing notes you posted. It's pretty easy—just click **Notes** (in the left menu) and then click **My Notes** below it. Notes you recently posted appear in reverse chronological order, and from here you can read and edit them.

You can also access your notes by heading to your Profile page and clicking the **Notes** tab. If you don't have a Notes tab, make one. Click the tab with the plus sign on it, and click **Notes.** Now whenever you want to view your notes, click **Profile,** then click the **Notes** tab.

Finding Out Who's Talking About You and What They're Saying

When posting a note, you and your friends have the option of tagging people mentioned in the note or those who might be interested in the note's content. Whenever a friend tags you in a note, you receive a notification, and the note appears in your Notes app and on your Wall. To view the note, click **Notes** (in the left menu) and then click **Notes About Me** under it. When you comment on a friend's note, it also appears on your My Notes page.

If you don't like what your friend has posted about you, or don't appreciate your friend tagging you in the note, you have two options:

- **Have your friend fix it:** Send your friend a message asking her to edit the note or remove the tag. This is usually the most prudent option because it educates your friend on what you think is acceptable. Your friend will know better next time.

- **Remove the tag:** You can remove the tag by clicking—you guessed it—**Remove Tag.**

Feeding Blog Posts into Notes

If you already maintain a blog, posting to the blog and then reposting your entries in Facebook can be a royal hassle. To avoid doubling your workload, consider setting up an RSS feed in Facebook that automatically pulls entries from your existing blog to display them as Facebook notes. Here's what you do:

1. From your Home page, click **Profile** (in the top menu) and then click your **Notes** tab. If you have no Notes tab, click the + tab and click **Notes.**

2. Under Notes Settings, click **Import a blog.** The Import an External Blog page appears, prompting you to type the address of your blog or RSS or Atom feed. If you don't see the **Import a blog** link, you may need to post several notes, as explained earlier in this chapter, first. After you've posted about ten notes, click **Profile,** click your **Notes** tab, scroll to the bottom, and click **See more notes.** You should then see the **Import a blog** link off to the right.

3. Click in the **Enter a website or RSS/Atom feed address** box and type the address of your blog or RSS or Atom feed, starting with **http://.**

4. Click the checkbox stating that you have the right to permit Facebook to reproduce the blog content.

5. Click **Start Importing.** Assuming everything works according to plan, Facebook displays a preview of the imported blog.

6. Check the preview, and if it looks okay, click **Confirm Import.** If it doesn't look okay, or you decide for whatever reason not to move forward with the import, click **Cancel.** Facebook returns you to the My Friends' Notes page.

7. Click **Profile** and then your **Notes** tab to view your newly imported blog posts.

If you decide later that you no longer want your blog entries to appear as notes, or you want to import entries from a different blog, you can remove the RSS feed. To do so, launch the **Notes** app and click **Edit Import Settings.** The Import a Blog page appears, displaying the address of the blog you're currently importing into Facebook. Click **Stop Importing.** Facebook displays a confirmation indicating that your feed was successfully removed.

 POKE

When you stop importing posts from a blog, this does not remove the blog entries that Facebook already imported. It simply prevents future blog entries from being added to your notes.

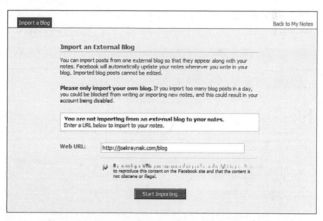

Enter the address of your blog or RSS/Atom feed.

The Least You Need to Know

- To launch the Notes app, head to your Home page, and then click **Notes** in the left menu.
- To share a friend's note by posting it to your News Feed and Wall, click the **Share** button for the note you want to share, and then click **Share** again.

- To post a note, launch the **Notes** app, click the **+ Write a Note** button, complete the **Write a New Note** form, and click **Publish.**

- To find out whether you've been tagged in any notes, click **Notes** (in the left menu) and click **Notes About Me.**

- If you maintain a blog, you can set up an RSS feed to have Facebook automatically import your blog entries and publish them on your Notes page.

Harnessing the Power of Facebook Applications

Without its apps (applications), Facebook is the stripped-down model of a social-networking utility. All you'd have left is the Wall, News Feed, and some Profile data. Add in Facebook's core apps, and you get the fully-loaded model, complete with photos, videos, notes, groups, links, events, and chat. All of these features are Facebook apps, which act as plugins to make Facebook so feature-rich.

But there's more. Facebook and third-party developers provide even more apps to enhance Facebook, including apps to play games, track your diet, share lists of your favorite books or movies, check your horoscope, send online greeting cards, shop or sell stuff, and even offer coupons to customers (if you're doing business on Facebook). In this part, we reveal all you need to know to app up.

Exploring More Facebook Applications

In This Chapter

- Recognizing a Facebook app when you meet one
- Exploring Facebook's massive apps collection
- Dealing with app security and privacy issues
- Tweaking your apps menu and bookmarks for easy app access
- Adjusting your Facebook app settings

Bet you didn't realize it, but you've already been using Facebook applications. Photos, Video, Groups, Events, Notes, Chat, Pages—they're all applications, or "apps" for short. These apps function as plugins for Facebook—accessories that enhance your experience. They add features that are not part of the core Facebook experience (although a few select apps, like Photos and Notes, are part of the core experience).

In this chapter, we introduce you to application basics, list the default apps, reveal where you can find thousands of apps on Facebook, and show you how to gain quicker access to the apps you use.

Grasping the Basics of Facebook Applications

Facebook apps can help you do all sorts of things—from playing games to tracking birthdays and anniversaries to movie reviews with friends. Facebook gives you access to thousands of apps, some of its own creations but mostly those created by third-party developers. Later in this chapter we'll show you how to search for specific apps and browse through Facebook's ever-growing collection of apps by category.

Fortunately, you have complete control over which apps you use or see. You can approve an app, block an app, or even bookmark apps as favorites for easy access. If a friend invites you to use an app, you're entirely free to accept or reject the invitation.

In the following sections, we introduce you to applications that function as core components of Facebook and show you how to search for specific apps and browse Facebook's complete collection. We'll also explain some of the security issues surrounding apps and how to deal with them.

Checking Out the Default Applications

You don't have to go hunting for apps to begin using them. Several apps are core functions in Facebook, including Photos, Video, Groups, Pages, Events, Notes, Links, Chat, and Gifts.

We've devoted a separate chapter to just about every core app on the list, except for Gifts. Gifts are sort of like greeting cards you send to your Facebook friends just to let them know you're thinking about them and wishing them well. You can send gifts on birthdays or anniversaries, when a friend is ill or has a baby, or on other special days, such as Valentine's Day, Independence Day, or Groundhog Day. Some gifts you can send for free, but for most, you have to purchase credits (using your credit card). In some cases, you can redeem your Facebook gifts for items in the real world, such as drinks at your local pub.

Digging Up More Applications

You're likely to discover plenty of apps through referrals as your friends use, recommend, and invite you to use popular apps. If that doesn't satisfy your app-etite, however, you can explore Facebook to gather more fun and useful apps.

Facebook has a well-stocked library of apps, which you can browse or search at any time. To search for an app, click in the **Search** box (in the top menu), type one or two words to describe the type of app you're looking for, and press **Enter.** Facebook displays a bunch of stuff that matches your search criteria, which may include groups, pages, and even friends. Click **Applications** (in the left menu) to narrow the search results to only apps.

If more than 10 apps matched your description, you'll find arrow buttons below the search results, which you can click to flip to the next and previous page of results.

You can search for specific apps or types of apps.

If you have no idea what you're looking for, you can browse the collection of apps. From your Home page, click **Applications** (left menu) to go to the Applications page. Scroll down to near the bottom to find app categories and subcategories. Read through the list to find the category or subcategory that's most likely to include the type of app you're looking for, and then click that category or subcategory.

A page appears that focuses on the category or subcategory you chose. The left menu enables you to choose a different category or subcategory. To the right of that menu apps in the selected category or subcategory appear, organized in three sections:

- **Featured by Facebook:** Facebook recommends several apps in the selected category you may want to check out. Use the right-arrow button just above the list to flip to the next page of featured apps.

- **Applications You May Like:** These are some of the most popular apps in the selected category.

- **Category Name:** The third section simply lists the applications in the selected category, initially by popularity—most to least popular. You can rearrange the list to show the newest applications first by clicking **Recently Added** in the bar at the top of this section. To see more of the apps in this category, click **See All** (on the right end of the section bar).

Evaluating and Authorizing Apps

Authorizing an app is like taking on a new friend—you want to make sure you trust the new app before approving it. While most apps are trustworthy and harmless (in addition to being fun or useful), some may take liberties with any information you allow it to access or even contact your Facebook friends on your behalf without your permission. So before you approve or authorize an app, do a background check to see what the app is all about and what other Facebook users have to say about it. (To control how much access apps have to your personal information, see Chapter 6.)

To perform a background check, head to the app's page. (Every app has its own page on Facebook.) To get to the page, click the app in Facebook's Applications area or click the link for the app wherever you happen to see it—in an App Request, your News Feed, or the Allow Access? box that pops up if you choose later to accept the app.

The Information box on the left contains the app's star rating (with a top rating of five stars), the number of Facebook members using the app, the number of your friends using the app, and an indication of whether the app was developed by Facebook (most are not).

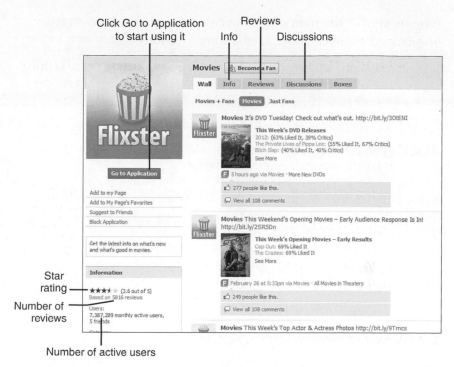

Every app has its own Facebook page.

To find out more about the app, you can click the link to read member reviews or click any of the options on the app's page to access Info, Reviews, and Discussions about the app. On the app's Wall, you can usually read additional information about new features or tips for using the app. Assuming plenty of Facebook members are using the app and it has a strong rating, numerous endorsements, and no or very few serious complaints about it, it should be pretty trustworthy.

If you like what you see, click **Go to Application** below the app's Profile picture to start using the app and then click **Allow** when prompted to allow access.

Addressing Security Concerns

Even if you don't use third-party apps, some of your information could be exposed to them through your friends' use. Information that apps can access includes your name, networks, list of friends, personal information, education and work history, and any other Profile information you share with the public. To restrict access to your information, you can adjust your privacy settings for applications as explained in Chapter 6.

Making Your Apps More Accessible

Facebook's core apps are already in easy reach—a mouse click away in the left menu. When you authorize an app, Facebook adds it to the Applications page, putting it two clicks away: click **Applications** (left menu) and then click the desired app. To give you more convenient access to your apps, you can bookmark an app, add it as a box or tab to your Profile, or add it to your browser's Favorites menu, as explained in the following sections.

Bookmarking an App

When you bookmark an app, Facebook displays an icon for it in the left menu under Applications, just below the icons for running the core apps. To bookmark an app, do one of the following:

- When using the app, click its **Add Bookmark** button. (Some apps may not have an Add Bookmark button.)

- Click **Account** (top menu), **Application Settings.** In the list of apps, next to the app you want to bookmark, click **Edit Settings.** In the resulting dialog box, click the **Bookmark** tab if necessary, click the check box to enable the **Bookmark** option, and then click the **Okay** button.

Add a Box or Tab to Your Profile

One of the best ways to store your apps in one convenient location is to add a box or tab for each app to your Profile. A tab provides the app with its own space, while any app you create a box for appears along with other boxed apps on your Profile's Boxes tab.

In addition to giving you quick access to your apps, placing the apps in your Profile offers an easy way to share apps with friends. Whenever they pull up your Profile, they can see which apps you're using, look at any gifts you've received, engage you in one of your favorite Facebook games, check out which books you've read and movies you've watched, and more (depending on which apps you've tabbed or boxed).

 POKE

Not all apps allow you to create a box or tab for them in your Profile. When you choose to change the app's settings, it may not have a Profile tab containing these options.

To add a tab or a box for an app, here's what you do:

1. Click **Account** (top menu) and then **Application Settings.** Facebook displays a list of apps you've recently used.

2. Next to the app you want to box or tab, click **Edit Settings.** A Settings dialog box pops up with the Profile tab in front, assuming the app supports boxes and/or tabs.

3. Next to **Box: Available** or **Tab: Available,** click **add.** If you chose to add a tab, Facebook adds it to your Profile. If this is the first app you boxed, Facebook adds a Boxes tab to your Profile and adds a box for the app to the tab.

You can add some apps to your profile without having to head to the Application Settings page. Just run the app and then click the option for adding it to your Profile.

You can rearrange boxes on your Boxes tab by dragging and dropping them. You can also shift the positions of the tabs you create by dragging and dropping them, but you can't move the standard tabs—Wall, Info, and Photos.

Responding to and Sending App Requests

As with most features on Facebook, apps are made to be shared. When a friend discovers an app she thinks is really cool (typically a game, a quiz, or a personality assessment), she shares it with her friends to encourage their participation. If a friend chooses to share an app with you, you receive an invitation that includes a brief description of the app.

In the following sections, you learn how to respond to an app request and send one of your own.

Responding to an App Request

When you receive an app request, the question for you is whether to authorize the app. You usually have two or three choices:

- **Accept:** App invitations always contain a button you can click to accept the invitation and authorize the app. The button is usually labeled Accept followed by the app's name or Join (or something similar) that indicates your desire to participate.

- **Learn More:** Some invitations include a Learn More button (or something similar) that displays more information about the app so you can make a well-informed decision about whether to give it the okay.

- **Ignore:** You can click the **Ignore** button to cancel the invitation without authorizing the app.

You can accept or ignore an app invitation.

Below the buttons, you have two more choices. You can click the **Block This Application** link to never again receive invitations for this particular application or click **Ignore All Invites from This Friend** to never again receive app requests from this particular friend. (When it comes to sending out app invites, some friends can be borderline spammers.) When the confirmation box pops up, simply click the button to confirm your desire to block the application or ignore all invites from your friend.

> **POKE**
>
> If you block an app and change your mind later, you can stop blocking the app. Click **Account** (in the top menu), click **Privacy Settings,** click **Applications and Websites,** click the **Edit Blocked Applications** button, and then click **Remove** next to the app you want to unblock.

You'll also see apps popping up on your News Feed or Live Feed, as a subtle invitation to participate. Assuming your friend hasn't disabled the News Feed and Wall notifications for apps, whenever he uses an app, a status update may appear in your News Feed and Live Feed indicating something related to your friend's interaction with the app. At the end of the post, you'll find the usual links to comment on the update or like it, along with another link to start using the app or some feature of it. Click the link to find out more about the app. Facebook displays some information about the app along with options to Allow or Leave Application.

Inviting Your Friends to Use an Application

You just discovered the coolest app on the planet and are eager to share your good fortune with your friends ... or at least some of them. You could e-mail your friends to let them know, but Facebook offers an easier way—sending out *app requests.*

> **NETIQUETTE**
>
> When it comes to sending app requests (or invitations), less is more. You may think FarmVille is the ultimate in social entertainment, but chances are pretty good that most of your friends would rather be doing something else. If you just can't help yourself, at least be selective in sending app requests. Send them only to friends you really think will appreciate them. If you choose to authorize an app and it prompts you to send invitations to friends, you can always click **Skip.**

To send an app request, head to the app's page and click the tab for inviting friends; the tab name varies so look for something like Invite or Friends. Click the name or photo of each friend you want to invite. (You can also send invitations to non-Facebook members by typing their e-mail addresses in the Invite by E-Mail Address box.) After you've selected all the people you want to invite, click the **Send Request** button.

Editing Applications

Depending on the app you authorize, Facebook gives you some freedom in tweaking the app's settings. For example, you can hide the Photos tab in your Profile, change the tab's privacy settings to limit access to it, or change the app's permissions to grant or revoke special privileges, such as sending you notifications when certain events occur.

To edit an app's settings, click **Account** (top menu), **Application Settings.** This displays a list of apps you recently used. Next to the app whose settings you want to adjust, click **Edit Settings.** A dialog box pops up with several options for controlling the app's accessibility and permissions. Options vary among apps. Enter your preferences, and then click the **Okay** button.

The app itself may offer additional settings via the app's interface. Look for an option labeled Settings or Profile Settings when you're using the app.

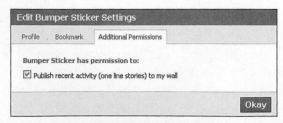

You can edit an app's settings to adjust its accessibility and permissions.

The Least You Need to Know

- You can access Facebook's core apps via the left menu.
- To hunt for more apps, click **Applications** (left menu), and use the resulting screen to search for or browse Facebook's massive app collection.
- Before authorizing an app, research its Facebook page to find out what other Facebook members have said about it.
- If you receive an app request from a friend, you have five options: Accept, Ignore, Learn More, Block This Application, and Ignore All Invites from This Friend.
- To tweak an app's settings, click **Account, Application Settings,** click **Edit Settings** next to the app you want to edit, and use the resulting dialog box to enter your preferences.

Playing Games with Friends and Strangers

In This Chapter

- Checking out the top games on Facebook
- Finding even more games to play
- Convincing friends to join in the fun
- Making new friends through games

A lot of people waste … er … *spend* a lot of time on Facebook playing all sorts of games, voting in polls, and taking personality tests like "Which flower represents you?" and "Which dead rock star are you?"

If you enjoy sharing in the revelry, this chapter introduces you to some of the most popular games and other distractions on Facebook, shows you how to find even more games and add them to your list of favorites, and explains how to engage others in a friendly game of whatever it is you enjoy playing. Games can be a great way to meet new friends and break the ice.

Oh, the Games People Play!

Social games on Facebook are all the rage, but different games appeal to different people. In addition, the popularity of certain games tends to rise and fall. When poker was all the rage, Texas Hold'Em Poker was one of the most popular games on Facebook, followed closely by Mafia Wars. After some time, however, people began leaving the card table for FarmVille, where they could manage their own virtual farms in cyberspace.

In the following list, you get to sample the games that made the top-10 list while we were writing the book. We'd wager that by the time you read this, some of these games won't make the cut, and new games will have risen to the top, but these top 10 give you a pretty good feel for the cross-section of social games available on Facebook.

1. **FarmVille:** On FarmVille, you till the soil, plant seeds and trees, harvest cash crops, build farmhouses and barns, milk cows, decorate, expand your farm, and even invest in farm machinery to make your job easier. Invite your Facebook friends to settle on neighboring farmland, and you can help them with their farms to earn extra points. If you get serious about this farming thing, you can pay real cash to buy game money that'll help you build your farm faster.

2. **MindJolt Games:** MindJolt Games is an ever-growing library of games you can play alone or with friends. Game categories include action, puzzle, strategy, shooter, sports, and style and are further divided into scored and unscored games. One of the most popular games in the collection is Bouncing Balls, in which you shoot balls out of a cannon to clear balls from the screen before the thousand-ton weight at the top reaches the bottom.

3. **Mafia Wars:** Mafia Wars is the flip side of FarmVille. Instead of toiling honestly on a farm, you start a mafia family with your friends, run a criminal empire, vie for respect, and fight to become the most powerful family in New York City. After reaching certain levels in the game, you get to travel to Cuba and Russia to increase your power and reach. You earn money and power by doing jobs and then robbing other mafia organizations.

4. **Texas Hold'Em Poker:** Zynga's popular poker game allows you to ante up with your friends and engage in one of the classic games of all time … Texas style. You start each day with a small stack of chips plus any winnings you have accumulated from previous games. If you have a credit card

handy, you can purchase more chips, or you can sign up for offers from companies to receive free chips. Unfortunately, you can't cash out that $5 million you won the night before.

5. **Farm Town:** Farm Town is almost identical to FarmVille. You start with some game coins you use to purchase and plant seeds. As you harvest and sell crops, you earn more coins to plant crops and hire workers to harvest crops for you. You can moonlight by helping your neighbors with their crops or enlist their help in harvesting your crops. As you move to higher levels, more options become available, including better cash crops.

6. **Pet Society:** In the world of Pet Society, you create your own virtual pet and then try to keep it happy by providing food, water, and treats; petting and grooming it; engaging in interesting outings and activities; furnishing its home; and competing in contests. Because this is a society, you get to meet and mingle with other pets as you explore this virtual world of pets.

7. **YoVille:** YoVille is Facebook's answer to *The Sims*. After launching the game, you become a Yo and proceed to customize your appearance—skin color, eye color, hair, clothing, you name it. You can then furnish and decorate your home and begin inviting other Yo's over to visit or visit them in their apartments. As you mingle with others, you can dance, kiss, joke, fight, or send messages and gifts. Through your interactions and the hours you put in at the YoVille Widget factory, you earn coins you can use to go shopping!

8. **Restaurant City:** In Restaurant City, you become the owner and operator of your own virtual restaurant, where you earn cash serving food, shaking the trees around your restaurant, and picking up the trash. With the cash you earn and other items you pick up while playing the game, you can visit the market to purchase ingredients for cooking and serving even more food. You can even hire workers and manage them, but be sure to let them rest occasionally or they get burned out.

9. **Bejeweled Blitz:** This addictive video game displays a grid of different colored gems and challenges players to rearrange them to line up three of the same gems in a row. Every time you line up three gems in a row, they disappear, and you score points. The game offers several ways to score bonus points, including a speed multiplier, power gems (when you align four in a row) that you can use to destroy the nine gems around it, and a hyper gem (when you align five in a row) that you can use to destroy all the gems of one color.

10. **Bumper Sticker:** Bumper Sticker is less like a game and more like a swap meet. Facebook members can view, upload, and share virtual bumper stickers with one another, display them in their Profiles and News Feeds, and stick them on a friend's Profile. You can browse through millions of quirky, fun, and funny bumper stickers or make one of your own!

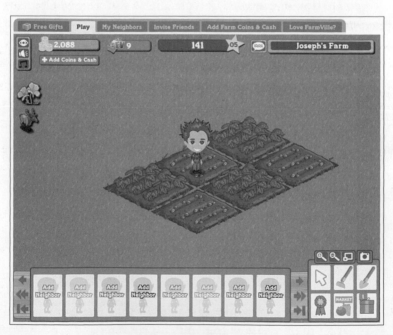

Plant and harvest virtual crops on FarmVille.

Finding Games on Facebook

Tracking down games on Facebook is as easy as tracking down apps, as explained in Chapter 13. In fact, games are apps. Although you can use the Search box in the top menu to perform a broad search for games, you're usually better off browsing Facebook's collection. To start browsing, head to your Home page and click **Games** (in the left menu). This takes you to the Games page, which is divided into six areas, only four of which have any importance when you're just getting started:

- **Friends' Recent Activity:** As your friends play games, their recent activities in those games appear here, subtly encouraging you to join in the fun.

- **Friends' Games:** If your friends play games on Facebook, those games appear in this section. Choosing a game one or more of your friends already play makes finding a playmate easier.

- **Game Categories:** Scroll down to the bottom of the page to browse Facebook's Games collection. Here you find links to games organized by category, including Action & Arcade, Board, Card, and Role Playing. Below each categories short list is a link to view more games in that category.

- **Featured:** In the upper-right corner of the Games page are a couple featured games you may want to check out.

Browse Facebook apps to find games.

Let's Play Already!

Every game is unique, so trying to provide instructions on how to play each one would be ridiculous. All we have room to cover are the basics—launching the game, inviting friends to play, and responding to invitations from friends.

 POKE

Unfortunately, game developers typically provide little or no guidance for new players to get up and running. You pretty much have to start playing and hope that on-the-job training is sufficient. You may be able to pick up a little guidance on the game's Application page. Just click the game's name wherever it appears as a link. If you have friends who've played the game, you can consult them. You can also search the web for instructions—sometimes players post basic instructions on sites such as eHow.com.

Launching a Game

Whenever you authorize a game, Facebook adds it to your Games page. When you're ready to play, click **Games** (left menu) and then click the game you want to play. Your games appear at the top of the list.

If you bookmark the game (see Chapter 13), you can start playing by clicking its icon in the left menu (below Applications). Or, if you tagged the game as a Favorite or Bookmark in your web browser (also discussed in Chapter 13), you can choose the game from your browser's list of Favorites or Bookmarks.

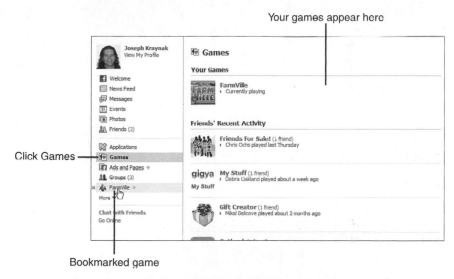

To play a game, click its name on the Games page.

Encouraging Your Friends to Play

The main purpose of social games is to socialize, so almost every game on Facebook is geared to engage friends in the fun. FarmVille, for example, constantly encourages players to spread the word and invite friends to play. The invitation can be something soft, such as posting a story to your News Feed announcing that you just won a Yellow Ribbon, or something more direct, like asking your friends to help you find a home for the new kitten that just wandered onto your property. You can also invite friends at any time by clicking **Add Neighbor** at the bottom of the screen.

However you choose to invite friends to play, an Invite Friends page pops up, prompting you to select from your list of friends. Click the friends you want to invite and click the button to send your invitation(s).

You can invite friends to join in the fun.

NETIQUETTE

Avoid the temptation to invite all of your friends to play the cool new game you just discovered. Invite only those friends you know enjoy playing games, and from that subset, select only the friends you strongly feel will enjoy playing *this* game. Invite the wrong person too many times, and she's likely to either block any of your future invitations or de-friend you.

Making New Friends Through Games

If you're having trouble finding friends to play your favorite game with you, consider joining a group devoted to the game. Check out Chapter 9 to learn more about groups and how to find and join groups. You're likely to find several groups packed with people eager to meet new players. In addition, your new friends can help bring you up to speed on the game and provide useful tips.

Responding to a Friend's Request to Play

When a friend invites you to play a game, you have five options:

- **Accept:** App invitations always contain a button you can click to accept the invitation. The button is usually labeled Accept followed by the name of the game or Join (or something similar) that indicates your desire to play.

- **Ignore:** You can click the Ignore button to cancel the invitation without authorizing the app.

- **Block This Application:** Click this link to never again receive invitations for this particular game.

- **Ignore All Invites from This Friend:** Click this link to never again receive game requests from this particular friend.

The Least You Need to Know

- Facebook games are social games, designed for group interaction.
- Some of the more popular Facebook games include FarmVille, Mafia Wars, and Texas Hold'Em Poker.
- To find games, head to your Home page and click **Games** (in the left menu), and then scroll down to the bottom of the Games page to browse Facebook's game collection by category.
- After authorizing a game, you can find it on your Games page.
- Be selective when inviting friends to play games. Not all of your friends will appreciate receiving game invitations.

Facebooking with Your Mobile Phone

In This Chapter

- Setting up Facebook Mobile to work with your phone
- Receiving and sending status updates remotely
- Uploading digital photos and video clips from your phone
- Taking Facebook on the road

When you leave your home or office or wherever it is you usually spend time on Facebook, you don't have to leave your friends behind. In fact, you might find that using Facebook on your mobile phone is actually more useful and fulfilling than on your laptop or desktop computer. Think about it; many of today's cell phones have built-in photo, video, and text capabilities, which is exactly why most people use Facebook—to share photos, status updates, and videos. Why wait until you're in front of your computer when you can do all of that and more right from your Facebook-enabled phone?

Assuming you have a cell phone, iPhone, or other such wireless device, you can text your status updates, view and upload photos and videos, check your Facebook messages, and (depending on the capabilities of your device) even run certain Facebook apps on the fly. This chapter takes you on the road with your mobile phone and shows you to how instantly update and stay up-to-date using Facebook's mobile features.

Setting Up Facebook Mobile

The first thing you need to do to use Facebook on a mobile phone is log in to your Facebook account and click the **Mobile** link at the bottom of any Facebook page, or visit www.facebook.com/mobile. Once there, you'll see any number of calls-to-action, including information about uploading photos via e-mail, updating your status from your phone, receiving News Feed items on your phone, and downloading Facebook applications built specifically for mobile phones. While all of these are interesting and useful, what you want to focus on right now is the **Edit Settings** link at the bottom of the page.

FRIEND-LY ADVICE

Make sure your cell phone is web-enabled. If you can browse the World Wide Web and send and receive text messages using your phone, you're all set. If, however, your cell phone isn't web-enabled or set up to send and receive text messages, you'll need to consult your wireless carrier about switching to a phone that allows you to use Facebook.

Clicking on the **Edit Settings** link brings up a page that allows you to register your mobile phone for Facebook Text Messages, which include status updates, Wall posts, messages sent to friends' Inboxes, and more. Follow these steps to get started:

1. Click **Register for Facebook Text Messages,** which opens a pop-up window asking you to choose your country and mobile service provider. (While most mobile providers support Facebook, some do not. If yours isn't on the list, Facebook Mobile won't work on your phone.)

2. Click the **Next** button and follow the on-screen instructions to send a text message containing only the letter "f" (without quotes) to 32665 (FBOOK).

3. Click the **Next** button, and then check your cell phone for a text message from Facebook containing your unique Facebook Mobile Activation Code.

4. Enter your Facebook Mobile Activation Code in the designated space.

5. Make sure the **Add my cell number to my Profile** option is clicked.

6. Click **Confirm.**

That's it. Your mobile phone is now activated to use Facebook Mobile, and you're ready to roll. Now you're all set to start receiving status updates. When reviewing friend requests, if your phone is authorized to accept messages from Facebook, you can click **Subscribe via SMS** to have friends' messages sent to your phone (on a friend-by-friend basis). Similarly, after your phone is set up to receive Facebook messages, you can click **Subscribe via SMS** under any friend's Profile picture.

Of course, Facebook Mobile enables you to do more than simply receive status updates. You can now post status updates, share photos and videos, send and receive Facebook messages, receive Wall posts, and use third-party applications that enhance your Facebook experience and productivity. Keep reading to tap the full potential of Facebook Mobile.

> **WHOA!**
>
> While Facebook doesn't charge for status updates, Wall posts, and messages, your mobile service provider does. Check your mobile rate plan before signing up to send messages and receive all your friends' status updates as text messages on your phone. As you'll see later in this chapter, if you're not on one of those all-inclusive plans, you may be better off using Facebook via your phone's web browser, if it's equipped with one.

Texting to Facebook

After you've activated your phone to send and receive Facebook status updates, Wall posts, and messages, performing those tasks is pretty easy. (And if you stop and think about it, posting status updates when you're out and about, when you're experiencing life and have more to say or sitting around twiddling your thumbs in a waiting room or airport, makes a lot more sense, too.) Most Facebook users post status updates only when they're sitting in front of their computers. We can't tell you how many times we've found the need—okay, it's really more of a *desire* than a need—to post status updates on the road, in the passenger seat of the car, at a restaurant waiting for a friend, sitting in the airport, or at a game where the most amazing thing just happened.

Having the flexibility to share interesting news, opinions, and observations with our Facebook friends whenever and wherever the spirit moves us is a real treat. Some business owners and leaders have come to consider it a necessity. In the following sections we show you how to use Facebook Mobile to access Facebook's most popular features when you're away from your computer.

Posting Status Updates

Using your mobile phone to keep your Facebook friends—and fans, if you use Facebook for your business, organization, or brand—updated on what you're thinking or up to is a snap. Once you've authorized your cell phone for Facebook Mobile, posting status updates from your phone is as simple as sending an SMS (short message service) to 32665 (FBOOK). Said differently, text a message—for example, "I'm reading *The Complete Idiot's Guide to Facebook;* you should, too!"—from your Facebook-enabled cell phone to 32665 and it will show up in your Facebook account as a status update.

But wait, there's more.

Texting Facebook Commands

Now that your phone is set up to send and receive messages from Facebook, you can:

- **Send a message to a Facebook friend:** Text **msg** followed by your friend's name followed by your message to 32665, and your text shows up in your friend's Inbox on Facebook. For example, "msg joseph kraynak running 45 min late."

- **Search for a friend's Facebook details:** Text **search [name]** to 32665, and you receive a text message from Facebook containing your friend's Facebook data, which usually includes at least a phone number and e-mail address. For example, "search Mikal Belicove" will result in receiving a message with Mikal's publicly available information on Facebook (assuming he's your friend).

- **Post a note on Facebook:** Text **note** followed by your note's content to 32665 and your note appears on Facebook and in your News Feed.

- **Post a message on a friend's Wall:** Text **wall** followed by your friend's name followed by your Wall post to 32665, and your message appears on your friend's Facebook Wall. For example, "wall Mikal Belicove Really enjoying *The Complete Idiot's Guide to Facebook*. Nicely done!"

- **Send a friend request:** Text **add** followed by your future Facebook friend's name to 32665 to send a friend request. For example, text "add Mikal Belicove" to send Mikal a friend request.

- **Become a fan:** Text **fan** followed by the name of the Facebook fan page to 32665 to instantly become a fan of a specific page on Facebook. For example, text "Idiot Book" to become a fan of our official page for the book.

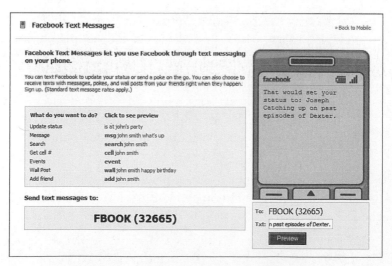

Facebook's text messaging simulator enables you to take text messaging for a test drive online.

As you can see, Facebook goes to great lengths to make it as easy as possible to get the most out of your Facebook text messaging experience. Using an online text message simulator, you can see what type of text messages you can send and receive using your Facebook-enabled cell phone. To access the simulator, head to www.facebook.com/mobile/?texts.

Uploading Photos and Videos from Your Phone

With a photo- or video-enabled cell phone and access to your own unique Facebook-specific e-mail address, you no longer need to download photos or videos to your home computer or laptop and then go through the steps outlined in Chapters 7 and 8 to upload them to Facebook. With Facebook Mobile, you simply shoot your photos and videos on your phone and upload them to Facebook via e-mail whenever you want.

To get started, locate and add your personalized Facebook e-mail address for mobile uploads. Here's how:

1. Click the **Mobile** link on the bottom of any Facebook page.

2. Look for the section titled **Upload via E-mail**. Here you'll find your personalized e-mail address for sending photos and videos to your Facebook Profile.

3. Copy and paste the e-mail address into your cell phone's e-mail program or text messaging address book and you're good to go. Or click the **Send me my upload e-mail** button to have Facebook text the address to your cell phone.

Uploading to Facebook from your cell phone is now easily accomplished by sending your photos and videos to your personalized Facebook e-mail address.

FRIEND-LY ADVICE

You can also use your personalized e-mail address for mobile uploads to upload photos and videos from your laptop or desktop computer. Simply attach your photos or videos to an outgoing e-mail message and send it to your personalized upload e-mail address as explained above.

When you upload via e-mail, whatever you type into your message's subject line automatically becomes the title of the video or the caption of the photo you're uploading.

After you've uploaded your photos or videos to Facebook, the uploaded items are automatically posted to your Profile. Photos show up in your Mobile Uploads album, which is accessible via your Photos tab, and video files are stored on your Video tab. We recommend editing uploaded photos and videos the next time you log in to Facebook, because the only content set for Mobile Uploads is the caption for photos and title for videos. See Chapter 7 for more on editing photos and Chapter 8 for information on editing videos.

Taking Facebook Mobile Web on the Road

If your cell phone can access the Internet and has a web browser, check out m.facebook.com from your phone's browser. Here you'll find Facebook Mobile Web, a version of Facebook that's optimized for cell phones with web browser capabilities.

If you're skeptical about how Facebook will look on a screen $\frac{1}{16}$ the size of a standard computer screen, we don't blame you. To help you overcome your skepticism, Facebook has built a nifty Mobile Web simulator that allows you to see what your Profile, Inbox, photos, and more will look like from a web-enabled cell phone using your laptop or desktop computer. Visit www.facebook.com/mobile/?web to take Facebook Mobile Web for a spin.

While Facebook Mobile Web works on the iPhone, Palm, BlackBerry, or any other web-enabled phone, other cell phone–specific versions of Facebook's interface do exist. For example, Facebook and Apple have combined efforts to create an iPhone version of the site, while Microsoft, Palm, and BlackBerry all have different versions depending on the make and model of your phone. Visit www.facebook.com/mobile for a complete and up-to-date list of what's available for your web-enabled cell phone.

Take Facebook Mobile Web for a spin with the simulator.

Most web-enabled cell phones allow you to access your Facebook Profile just as you would from your laptop or desktop computer. Some differences do exist, however, so you'll want to download the version that's made for your cell phone and see which features work for you and your on-the-go Facebook needs.

The Least You Need to Know

- If your cell phone is web-enabled, you can use it to access your Facebook account when you're on the road.

- To set up Facebook Mobile for your cell phone, head to www.facebook.com/mobile, click **Edit Settings,** and follow the on-screen instructions.

- To post a status update from your cell phone, send a text message to 32665 (FBOOK).

- To post a message on a friend's Wall, text **wall** followed by your friend's name followed by your Wall post to 32665.

- To obtain a personalized Facebook e-mail address for mobile uploads, click the **Mobile** link at the bottom of any Facebook page.

Shopping and Selling in Facebook's Marketplace

In This Chapter

- Getting to Facebook's Marketplace
- Browsing and searching the listings
- Contacting the seller
- Posting a listing to sell, trade, give stuff away, or ask for stuff

Marketplace is an online classifieds area where you can connect with members to buy, sell, trade, give stuff away, and even ask for stuff sort of like Craigslist. In addition, you can peruse the job listings or post a job opening. While nonmembers can view your listings, the only way they can respond to your listing is to become a Facebook member, which provides some degree of safety. You discover how to do all this and more right here, as we lead you through the aisles of the Marketplace.

Going to Market

You might assume that Facebook's Marketplace is like most markets—centrally located and easy to find. Unfortunately, you'd be wrong. According to the product manager for Marketplace, the only road leading to Marketplace (at the time this book was written) runs through the Applications menu. No button or link on the member's Home page leads to it, so you have to search Facebook's apps collection.

1. Click in the **Search** box (top menu), type "marketplace," and press **Enter.** (Marketplace should appear at the top of the page under Applications. If it doesn't, click **Applications** in the left menu.)

2. Click **Marketplace.** The Marketplace Home page appears.

3. Click **Go to Application.** Marketplace appears.

Once you find the Marketplace, you can bookmark it or add it as a favorite in your web browser for quick access. See Chapter 13 for details.

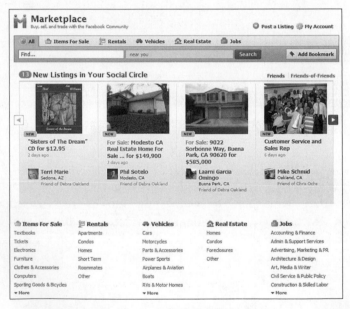

Facebook's Marketplace.

Checking Out the Listings

Although Marketplace has tens of thousands of listings at any one time, they're searchable and browseable by category, making them much easier to navigate and find what you're looking for. In addition, you can trim the search results even more by narrowing your focus geographically.

> **WHOA!**
>
> Shopping Facebook's Marketplace may be a little safer than shopping in more open markets (like Craigslist), but no marketplace is completely safe. Take precautions. Never send money to anyone you don't fully trust. Always meet the seller in person so you know the person you're dealing with. And if it sounds too good to be true, it probably is.

Browsing by Category

When you're not really sure what you're looking for, or are more interested in window-shopping than buying, you can browse the Marketplace listings by category. Marketplace arranges listings in four major categories: Items for Sale, Rentals, Vehicles, Real Estate, and Jobs. Below most categories is a list of subcategories, and you can click **More** at the bottom of the list to view the remaining subcategories.

To start browsing, click the category or subcategory of interest. A list of items in the selected category or subcategory, and in the geographical area you specified, appears.

Click a category or subcategory to start browsing.

Searching for Specific Items

When you know what you want, browsing is an unnecessary hurdle standing between you and your object of desire. To clear this hurdle, click in the **Find** box and type a brief description of what you're looking for. By default, Marketplace will display search results near you, as determined by the city and state listed in your Profile. To broaden the search or choose a different location click the **near you** box, choose a country, range, and Zip code, and click **Submit.** To execute the search, click the **Search** button. Marketplace displays a list of items matching your description near you or in the geographical area you specified.

Narrowing Your Search

Whether you're browsing or searching, you may discover so many items you may not know where to start. Fortunately, whether you're searching or browsing for stuff, Marketplace displays several options on the left for narrowing the list of items:

- **Location:** Click the **Location** box to display the Location Settings dialog box, in which you can select a country, a range (X miles from the specified Zip code or the entire country), and specify a Zip code.

- **Friends & Networks:** If you really don't want to deal with strangers, click **Filter by Friends and Networks.**

- **Keyword:** To zero in on a specific item, type a descriptive word or two in the **Keyword** box and press **Enter.**

- **Subcategory:** Click a subcategory to view only items listed in that subcategory.

- **Price:** Under Price, type a low number in the **Low** box and the top price you're willing to pay in the **High** box and press **Enter.**

If you overfilter, you can remove one or more of the criteria you used to filter the list. Just click the **X** next to the filter you want to remove.

POKE

The Friends and Networks filter is often referred to unofficially as the "weirdo filter." Assuming you're getting items only from people you know, you tend to eliminate the weirdos who list items as a way to prey on unwary shoppers.

Responding to a Listing

When you happen upon a listing that catches your interest, click its title or photo to display the item on its own page with additional information and/or photos. You can then respond to the listing in any of the following ways:

- **Contact the seller:** Click the **Respond** button and use the resulting form to send a message to the seller about this item.

- **Comment on the item or listing:** Post a comment about the item or the listing. Your comment will appear with the full item listing.

- **Vote your approval:** Click **Like** to give the item the thumbs up and help spread the word about it by having your Like posted in your News Feed, which makes it eligible to show up in your friends' News Feeds.

- **Share the listing with your friends:** If you think one or more of your Facebook friends will like the listing, click **Share** to post the listing in your News Feed or send it via Facebook message to one or more friends.

Posting Your Own Listing

Whether you have something to sell or give away or are looking for a particular item or even a job, you can turn to Facebook's Marketplace for help. In a matter of minutes, you can create a listing complete with a description and photos and post it in the Marketplace for all to see.

 WHOA!

Posting is forever. After you post a listing, it remains in the Marketplace. You can edit a listing at any time, or close a listing so it's no longer active, but you can't delete a listing.

Sell It, Give It Away, or Ask for It

Whenever you post a listing, Marketplace gives you three options. You can sell it, give it away, or ask for it. Assuming you have something in mind that matches one of those descriptions, head to the Marketplace and click **Post a Listing** (in the upper right of the Marketplace). The Post an Ad – Details dialog box appears. Enter your geographical location (country along with city and state or Zip code), choose the category in which you want the item posted, and click **Post.** The dialog box expands, prompting you for additional details.

Complete the dialog box to enter all required information and any optional information to include in the listing, including a subcategory for the listing; a title and description; whether the item is for sale, free, or something you want; and how much money you want for the item (if any). You can also upload a photo of the item, which always helps generate more interest in it. When you're done entering details, click **Post** to post the item in the Marketplace.

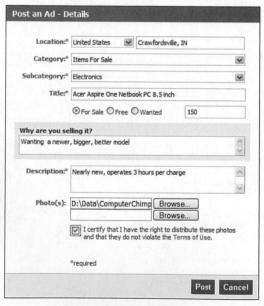

Start by posting the item.

After you submit the listing, Marketplace displays a dialog box asking whether you want to notify your friends by sharing the listing in your News Feed and posting it to their Home pages. Click the option you feel is best. Notifying your friends helps spread the word and increase your chances of success, but some friends may not appreciate receiving the notification.

When you're done, Marketplace displays your full listing so you can review and edit it, if necessary.

Viewing and Tweaking Your Listings

After posting a listing, you may notice it contains typos or the photos don't look quite right. Even worse, your listing may not be generating any interest. Whatever the case, you want to check out your listing and perhaps make a few adjustments. Fortunately, your listing is only a couple clicks away. Just head to Facebook's Marketplace and, in the upper right, click **My Account.** This displays a page with any and all of your listings. To view the full listing, click the listing title or photo. To edit the listing, click **Edit Details.**

You can edit your listing at any time.

If you click **Edit Details,** a dialog box pops up that looks almost identical to the dialog box you used to create the listing. Edit the information as desired. To delete a photo, mouse over the photo and click the red **X** that appears in its upper-right corner. You can also upload new photos, if desired.

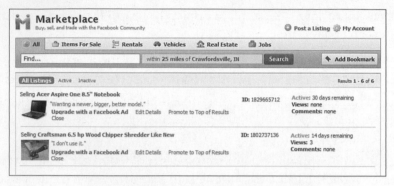

Facebook displays all of the listings you posted.

On the My Listings page are several links for other options. If you have numerous listings, you can narrow the list by clicking **Active** (to view only active listings) or **Inactive** (to view only inactive listings). For each listing, you can also click **Promote to Top of Results** so your listing will republish at the top of users' search results for that item. You can also close a listing, as explained in the following section.

Closing a Listing

After you've sold whatever you were selling or received whatever you were looking for, you should close the listing so Facebook members won't waste time looking at it and asking questions and you won't waste time answering them. To close a listing, head to Marketplace, click **My Account,** and in the listing you want to close click **Close.** A dialog box appears, indicating that your listing will be removed momentarily and the screen will refresh showing that the listing has been closed. Click **OK.**

The Least You Need to Know

- To find the Marketplace for the first time, click in the **Search** box (top menu), type "marketplace," and press **Enter.**

- You can browse the Marketplace by category or search for specific items.

- If your search turns up too many items, use the filters to the left of the list to filter the list.

- For safer shopping, consider narrowing your search to only those items listed by your friends or people in your networks.

- To respond to a listing, click the listing's title or photo, click the **Respond** button, and use the resulting form to send the seller a message about it.

- To post your own listing, head to the Marketplace, click **Post a Listing** (upper right), and use the resulting dialog box to create, post, and share your listing.

Getting Down to Business on Facebook

4

Doing business on Facebook is sort of like selling raffle tickets at a family reunion. People gather on Facebook to socialize, not to buy stuff, and they don't appreciate being blasted with ads or sales pitches. Yet most Facebook users expect businesses and organizations to have a presence in the community and provide something that engages and benefits the community—typically valuable, relevant information.

In this part, we try to sell you on the idea of doing business on Facebook, and we show you how to use Facebook's advertising features to do business in a way that can lift sales, increase customer retention, and attract new customers without turning off the people you're trying to impress.

Doing Business in a Social Setting

In This Chapter

- Recognizing the business potential of Facebook
- Incorporating Facebook advertising in your marketing campaign
- Getting customers involved with Groups
- Avoiding the most common pitfalls

Selling effectively in a social setting requires a huge paradigm shift from traditional marketing, advertising, and sales. On Facebook and other social-networking sites, establishing credibility and trust and building relationships take precedence over making a sale. Companies and brands that succeed are rewarded through positive word-of-mouth advertising and referrals. Those who ruffle the feathers of too many Facebook members feel their wrath as the negative publicity spreads almost instantly.

In this chapter, we make the case for implementing Facebook in your promotional efforts, introduce you to features designed specifically for this purpose, and provide tips on how to do business most effectively on Facebook.

The Business Case for Facebook

If we told you 400,000,000+ people were happily gathered in one central location online—many of whom are your customers and prospective customers—and that the majority of them expect to see your business or brand there, wouldn't you want to be there, too? In a nutshell, that's the case for promoting your business or brand on Facebook. With millions of consumers using this one über–social–networking platform to connect with friends and interact with others around topics that interest them, your business has a tremendous opportunity to gain powerful access to the very people who fill your coffers.

Unlike banner, e-mail, and pay-per-click advertising (push-marketing tactics, in which you push your message to the masses and wait for a direct response), setting up shop for your business on Facebook is a highly effective pull strategy. When done correctly, it enables you to engage with your customers—and engagement is what Facebook is all about.

With engagement comes the possibility of word-of-mouth advertising, which, of course, is nothing new. What is new is that the Internet has become the breeding ground for the placement and distribution of user-generated content—and not just the funny sound your cat just made. Users talk about businesses and products, ask and answer questions, post and read reviews, share rip-off stories about bad experiences they've had with certain companies, and sing the praises of top-notch businesses and quality brands.

Facebook expands the reach of word-of-mouth advertising and the speed at which it spreads, and it has quickly become the platform of choice for businesses and their customers to connect and engage online. Regardless of whether your business has a presence on Facebook, chances are that your customers do, so you should be there, too.

FRIEND-LY ADVICE

At the end of the day, marketing on Facebook is still marketing, so don't abandon everything you already know about marketing. You simply need to know how to apply your marketing savvy and expertise to Facebook.

Tapping the Power of Facebook Advertising

Most users know that businesses and organizations can advertise on Facebook. Glance at the right side of nearly any Facebook page and you'll see at least one ad. What many businesses and organizations fail to realize, however, is that several of Facebook's advertising features are free. In the following sections, we introduce you to both the free and paid advertising offerings and reveal how you can use them alone or together to rev up your promotional efforts on Facebook.

Establishing a Base of Operations on a Facebook Page

Every business needs a home, and on Facebook the home of choice for a business or brand is its Facebook page. Pages are meant for businesses and brands to share news, opinions, and information about their products and services with Facebook members. Packed with available features that enable your business to engage with *fans* (members who choose to follow your page), Facebook pages allow you to build relationships, which often lead to positive word-of-mouth advertising and brand evangelism.

By posting timely and clever status updates, which show up in fans' News Feeds, businesses on Facebook find they're able to keep customers and prospects well informed of company news, events, contests, special offers, and more, as well as drive traffic back to their websites.

Before Facebook, if you wanted to reach out to customers to inform them of, say, a contest, you relied on e-mail or newsletters, which many people find more annoying than engaging. With a Facebook page, a business can post a status update announcing a contest, and chances are fairly good that a fan will leave a comment, which can spark a chain reaction. The comment gets published in the fan's News Feed for all his friends to see and inspires other fans to respond with their own comments, which in turn further promotes the contest.

If you're a business owner or marketing manager focused on your return on investment (ROI) from engaging with customers and others (which we like to refer to as ROE—return on engagement), you'll be glad to know that Facebook pages come complete with a suite of free tools that enable you to measure how many fans interact with your page, how old they are, where they live, and more.

In short, if you have something to promote, build a page. We show you how in Chapter 18.

Cross-Promoting Facebook on Your Blog or Website

Facebook presents the classic "if you build it, will they come" conundrum. On the one hand, your customers or brand advocates may think to search for you on Facebook, and if they do happen to find your page, they're likely to become fans. On the other hand, while the majority of Facebook members expect your business or organization to have a presence on Facebook, they rarely, if ever, search for you. Rather, they affiliate because of something you've done to inform them of your Facebook page, like posting a "find us on Facebook" badge on your website or blog or sending a special e-mail message to them announcing your new Facebook page. (In Chapter 18, we show you how to create a badge for your page.)

Cross-promotion is crucial to building a fan base on Facebook. Take every opportunity to let your customers know about your Facebook page and why they should want to become fans. If you run a retail storefront, restaurant, or office, print up some postcards or small fliers announcing your Facebook address, and make sure everyone receives one on their way out the door. Add a Facebook badge to your company e-newsletter, all of your e-mail marketing communications, and, of course, your website and blog. Heck, you might even go so far as to print your Facebook address on the company letterhead! If it works, go for it. Do anything you can to build a following on Facebook.

Posting Ads on Facebook

If all this "engagement" stuff has got you scratching your head and wondering whether you can just post an ad on Facebook promoting your products or services, then Facebook ads are for you. With 400,000,000+ active users, all of whom have supplied Facebook with their geographic and demographic information, Facebook ads allow you to reach only the people you want to target.

Suppose you're a wedding photographer and you only want to target your ad toward women in a certain locale between the ages of 24-30 whose relationship status is Engaged. Well, on Facebook, you can. Similarly, if you own the hip new sushi restaurant in town, you can target your ads toward a specific demographic, and if you run a Colorado-based not-for-profit that takes high school kids on back-country trips, you can target local or national wilderness enthusiasts to make a donation to your cause.

To learn more about Facebook ads, check out Chapter 19.

Going Viral with Facebook Connect

Through status updates, notes, photos, videos, and more, your business can create quite an impressive presence on Facebook. But what if you're BlackPast.org, the Google of African American History, with nearly 4,000 pages of content crying out to be shared with Facebook fans? Copying and pasting all that content into individual notes or attempting to create a status update calling attention to each one of your web pages would be a nightmare, even for an intern! The solution to your problem (actually, more opportunity than problem) may be *Facebook Connect*.

Think of Facebook Connect as a programming tool that allows your website programmer to add certain Facebook features—like Share, Comment, Recent Friend Activity, and more—to your website. So in the example above, BlackPast.org can add Facebook's Share button to each of its 4,000 or so pages, which encourages its visitors to recommend its content to all their Facebook friends.

There's a lot more you can do with Facebook Connect. To see for yourself, click on the **Advertising** link at the bottom of any Facebook page, then click **Connect** at the top of the next page.

> **FRIEND-LY ADVICE**
>
> Implementing Facebook Connect on your website isn't for amateur website builders. It requires tapping into Facebook's API (application programming interface), which is best handled by skilled and creative website developers, engineers, and programmers.

Establishing a Following with Groups

Another option that businesses, brands, and organizations have for connecting and engaging with Facebook members is to create a Facebook group. While groups have a similar look and feel to pages, Facebook intends for them to serve different purposes. While pages are managed by businesses or brands, groups are managed by Facebook members and are great for connecting with high school classmates, organizing family members for a reunion or Mom's surprise seventy-fifth birthday party, generating discussion among book club members, and so on.

While Facebook groups tend to be started and managed by individuals, that doesn't mean they can't be used for business purposes. Because they can be set as private/for members only, creating a group and inviting select business customers and brand advocates to join and engage with one another is a great way to facilitate focus groups and gain valuable insight into customer wants and needs.

Similarly, you can join groups that focus on topics related to your business or brand—assuming they are open to all Facebook members—and listen in to what people are saying. If appropriate to the situation, you can even respond officially as a company representative.

For more information on Facebook groups, check out Chapter 9, where we show you how to join a group, form groups of your own, engage in group discussions, and share stuff with fellow group members.

Engaging Members with Facebook Applications

Suppose you wanted your customers to be able to use your company website to share video testimonials about your business, photos of themselves using your products or services, or daily updates of their related activities. You'd spend a fortune designing, programming, and engineering your site to handle the activity and resulting traffic. With Facebook, that's all handled for you, and it doesn't cost you a cent.

Facebook's core applications—which include status updates, photos, and video—are all available for you to use for business purposes. Want to hold a contest to see who can create the best video featuring your products or services? With Facebook's video application, your customers can upload user-generated video files to Facebook and post them to your page's Wall, and you can call attention to them through status updates and notes.

With a little creativity, you're sure to figure out how your business can leverage Facebook's applications for business purposes. Let's say you run a chain of florist shops and you want your customers on Facebook to be able to send their Facebook friends virtual flower arrangements. By doing so, you think you're placing your flower shop in an enviable position of enabling virtual flowers to be sent back and forth on Facebook, and in the process will gain valuable visibility among people most inclined to send real flowers later on.

Great idea! But—because Facebook doesn't have a suitable application of its own—you'd have to build a virtual flower application, which would be required to meet Facebook's standards and guidelines for applications. Sound complicated? It is, which is why you should work with a professional Facebook application developer—someone who's successfully built Facebook apps before and knows her way around Facebook's development landscape.

Although Facebook doesn't provide a list of recommended application developers, you can find them by Googling "Facebook app developer" or checking out the Facebook application called Application Developer Services, which showcases and allows you to connect with developers of existing Facebook apps.

Do's and Don'ts of Doing Business on Facebook

If you're not careful, social-media marketing, particularly on Facebook, can do more harm than good. Going viral goes both ways: say the right thing, and the good word can spread like wildfire; say the wrong thing, and you'll be engulfed by that wildfire. To improve your odds of success, adhere to the following do's and don'ts of marketing on Facebook:

- **Do engage with your fans.** When a fan leaves a comment on one of your status updates, thank him, answer his question, or comment back (if appropriate). If a fan posts a photo or video on your Wall, make a comment or click the **Like** button if, indeed, you appreciate the post.

- **Do be authentic and transparent.** We live in the age of reality, where everyone feels they're entitled to know everyone else's business. (You can thank reality TV and cable news for that.) On Facebook, the same holds true for your business. If you launch a Facebook page, fans expect you to be real, and that means transparent and authentic. No hidden agendas allowed.

- **Don't self-promote too much.** Remember, it's called social networking, not social selling. While your customers expect you to be on Facebook, they don't expect you to take up all their time with advertisements and sales pitches.

- **Do choose a great Profile image.** Make sure it accurately and appropriately shows who or what you are. For most businesses, this means posting the company logo or an image of its brand-defining product or service.

- **Don't use "I" statements in status updates or notes.** A business is not an I, it's a we. If you post a status update about exhibiting at a conference or trade show, you wouldn't say, "I am exhibiting at such-and-such show later this week. Stop by and see me in booth number 513." Rather, you'd write something like, "Acorn Products will be exhibiting at such-and-such show later this week. Stop by and see us in booth number 513."

- **Do fill out your Profile.** Be complete, and include everything you're asked to provide in your Profile. Don't leave your fans—your customers and prospects—hanging. Give them all the information they need.

- **Don't create multiple pages for multiple products.** You may not have the resources to keep all the pages up-to-date and relevant.

- **Do create and post notes.** Like entries on company blogs, Facebook notes have the potential to be indexed by search engines, which means your notes—if packed with great keywords and phrases, and relevant to your business reason for being on Facebook in the first place—can help attract more fans and traffic.

- **Do choose a vanity URL.** Facebook allows page owners to request a specific URL for each of their pages. So rather than live with the Facebook-generated URL, which usually contains a series of numbers and symbols that are difficult to remember, you can tell customers to find you on Facebook at Facebook.com/yourcompanyname. (To obtain a vanity URL, your page must have a certain number of fans, and Facebook must approve your request. More about this in Chapter 18.)

- **Don't go long stretches without posting a status update.** Fans and passersby have a reasonable expectation that your Facebook page is going to be kept up-to-date, and the number one way of doing that is to create and post a consistent stream of status updates. One update per day is ideal, but if you can't do that, one every other day should suffice.

- **Don't put all your eggs in one Facebook basket.** Facebook is not the be-all, end-all marketing vehicle. It's just one more weapon in your marketing arsenal.

- **Don't forget everything you already know about marketing.** Facebook is just like every other marketing channel—you have to know your audience and what's considered the most acceptable way of communicating with that audience in that particular channel.

- **Do measure your efforts.** ROI on Facebook comes by way of ROE (return on engagement). Areas to measure include website traffic from Facebook, search engine results and ranking, inbound links to your website, number of fans or group members, comments on status updates, and mentions of your brand as a result of your Facebook-related activity.

The Least You Need to Know

- The business case for Facebook? 400,000,000+ people happily gathered in one central location online, many of whom are your customers and expect to see your business or brand there.
- At the very least, your business should have its own page to function as its base of operations on Facebook.
- Cross-promote your Facebook page and company website to drive traffic to each.
- Facebook ads give you the power to target Facebook users by locale and demographic.
- Use groups and business apps to further engage customers and prospects on Facebook.

Launching a Business-Based Page

In This Chapter

- Grasping the marketing potential of a Page
- Building and customizing a Page
- Keeping your page fresh with relevant, compelling content
- Attracting traffic
- Tracking results with Page Insights (analytics)

As a business or organization, you can establish a presence on Facebook by creating and customizing your very own Pages. A Page is a public Profile that enables you to share your business or organization and any products or services you offer with Facebook members.

Your Page can function as the central location for your business on Facebook, or you can use Pages to highlight very specific products or services— using them as you might use landing pages on the web. Through your Pages, you can post status updates to keep current and prospective customers informed and up-to-date. If your business or organization has a blog, you can even set up a feed on your Page that automatically pulls blog posts onto the Page.

Build a quality Page, populate it with relevant and compelling content, and begin to attract fans. When fans interact with your Page, these interactions can appear in their News Feeds, where their friends can find out about your Page and business and help spread the word. Do it right, and you may be able to spark a word-of-mouth promotional wildfire that advertises for you! In this chapter, we show you how.

The Business Case for a Page

In Facebook's early childhood, the entrance fee for establishing a business presence on Facebook excluded all but the richest corporations. Now any company or organization can launch a Facebook Page for free in a matter of minutes and use the Page as a launch pad for an effective social-media marketing campaign.

In Chapter 17, we make a case for doing business on Facebook. The same rationale applies to creating a Facebook Page. In fact, if you've decided to do business on Facebook, creating a Page for your business and/or the products and services you're selling is a no-brainer. Pages are free, they provide a base of operations, and they allow you to take the lead in discussions revolving around your business or organization and any products or services you offer.

POKE

Organizations, products, or services that have a strong brand presence often find that they're already on Facebook. Facebook members may create their own Facebook Groups or Pages where they discuss an organization's merits (or shortcomings) or discuss its products or services. This can be very positive for your organization, but you should still launch an official Page of your own so you can play more of a leadership role in any associated communities. You can then invite members of the other communities, who have already expressed an interest in your offerings, to become fans of your Page.

Crafting and Customizing Your Page

Your Page is your business's or organization's face on Facebook, so you want it to create a good and lasting first impression. You want people who see it to become fans so you can communicate with them directly. In the following sections, we show you how to lay the groundwork for a quality Page and then step you through the process of creating it.

Laying the Groundwork

Just because Facebook Pages are free to create doesn't mean they should look cheap. You should invest at least as much time preparing to create a Page as you would spend on creating a quality advertisement for your organization. Prior to creating a Page, make sure the following pieces are in place:

- **Purpose:** A Page without a purpose usually lacks impact.

- **Page name:** Settle on a name for your Page that customers and prospects are likely to recognize. You can't change the Page name later, so pick the right name the first time. Remember, you're trying to create brand identity, so consistency is key—the name should match whatever name you use offline.

- **Quality images:** Strictly speaking, images are optional, but if you want to appeal to the masses, you'd better use a high-quality image (something that puts a face on your business or organization) for your Profile picture. This may be your organization's logo or a photo of the number one product you're showcasing.

- **Content:** Content is key in turning fans into customers and customers into fans.

Generally speaking, the main goal of your Page should be to convince visitors to become fans and engage with your business or organization on Facebook. You may also have a secondary goal, such as encouraging Facebook members to visit your organization's website, keep fans in the loop concerning newsworthy events, gather insight into customer wants and needs, or inform fans of special deals and offers on your products and services. Your ultimate goal may be to sell, but when it comes to Facebook, selling should not be the purpose—warming up prospects and customers, creating community, and building trust are foremost.

If your company manufactures aftermarket parts for motorcycles, you may want to post announcements of upcoming races or rallies, videos showing how to install products, and photos of your parts on cool-looking bikes. If you're a restaurant, posting your menu, phone number, address, and a map of your location may be a good idea. Or you might want to post a much sought-after recipe that you're comfortable sharing with the public or a link to a great review in a local magazine or newspaper. If you're promoting a film, you'll want to include a trailer and create an event promoting the movie's premier. If you run a bed and breakfast in southern Vermont, you'll want to post ski conditions for the local resort, notices of availability, and specials on rooms in the off-season. Whatever you want to include, have it ready when you begin creating your Page. More details on populating your Page with relevant and compelling content are provided later in this chapter.

Focus your efforts on serving the community rather than your own interests. Posting your entire product catalog is probably a bad idea, because it sends a clear message that all you're interested in is selling products and collecting money. Posting a tip on how customers can enhance their experience with a particular product would be much better.

 POKE

Remember, it's called *social networking,* not *social selling.* While 90 percent of Facebook members expect businesses and organizations to have a presence on Facebook and other social-networking platforms and services, only 25 percent want to be marketed to. Facebook members prefer evangelizing brands themselves over being sold to.

Creating Your Page

The process of creating a Page is relatively easy. You click a link, enter your preferences and content via a series of forms, and your Page is up and running. The following list leads you through the process step by step:

1. Scroll to the bottom of the Facebook screen you're on (down to the footer) and click **Advertising.** The Advertising offerings appear.

2. Click **Pages** at the top of the page. The Facebook Pages screen appears.

3. Click the **Create a Page** button.

4. Do one of the following depending on the type of Page you're creating:

   • Click **Local business** and then select the category that best describes your business.

   • Click **Brand, product, or organization** and then select the category that most closely represents the brand, product, or organization you want to promote.

   • Click **Artist, band, or public figure** and then select the title that most closely represents the artist, band, or public office you're trying to promote.

5. Click in the **Page name** box and type the name you decided on in the previous section.

6. Click the checkbox next to "I'm the official representative of this person, business, band, or product and have permission to create this Page."

7. Click **Create Official Page.** Facebook creates and displays a blank Page, so you can add pictures, text, and other content.

8. Hover the mouse over the big **?** in the upper-left corner of the Page, click **Change Picture,** click **Upload a Picture,** and then upload the image you want to use to represent this Page. (For more about uploading photos and other images, see Chapter 7.)

9. Click **Write something about** followed by your page name (below the Profile picture) and type a brief but detailed description of whatever the Page is about. If you're promoting yourself, this can be about who you are, what you do, and your areas of expertise. If you're using the Page to promote a product, write a blurb about it that's likely to whet people's appetites.

10. Click the **Info** tab, click **Edit Information** (off to the right on the Info page), and enter basic and detailed information about yourself or your company, website, products, services, mission, and so forth as you wish. Clicking a bar, such as Detailed Info expands the section to display its options. (The available fields vary according to the category and subcategory you selected in Step 4.) When you're done, click **Save Changes.**

11. Post status updates or other content at least three times a week to attract fans and keep them engaged. You can post status updates to the Page's Wall, or post photos, videos, events, and notes on separate tabs. More details on populating your Page with relevant and compelling content are provided later in this chapter.

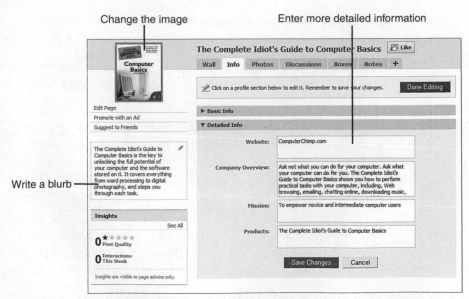

Flesh out your Page with an image and text.

Getting Back to Your Page

After creating your Page, you can always return to it to make changes. Regardless of what you're doing in Facebook, click on **Home** (in the top menu), then **Ads and Pages** (in the left menu). What happens next varies:

- If you have only one Page, settings for that Page show up as described in the following section. Click the **View Page** link to display the Page on a screen where you can edit its content.

- If you have two or more Pages, they appear in a list. Click the title of the Page you want to edit. You may need to click the **Info** tab to view and edit the information on the Page.

Another quick way to access your Page(s) is via the **Advertising** link at the bottom of any Facebook screen. Click **Advertising,** and then click **Pages** (at the top) followed by the **or manage your existing Pages** link under the **Create a Page** button.

Adjusting Your Page Settings

Immediately after creating your Page, check its settings and adjust them if necessary to control how your Page operates and shares information. To pull up your Page settings, head to the Page and then click **Edit Page** (below the photo box).

To edit any of the settings, click the **Edit** link for the settings you want to change. You can adjust the following:

- **Settings:** These options enable you to limit access to your Page to only the countries you specify, set a minimum age for accessing the Page, or change the Page's published status. Also, and this is very important, since Facebook's default setting for the Page's status is "Published (publically visible)," consider changing it to "Unpublished (visible to no one but admins)" until you are ready for the world to see your new creation.

- **Wall Settings:** Use these options to control access to the Page's Wall. You can specify whether you want only the Page to be able to post to the Wall or the Page and its fans, choose which tab first appears whenever a visitor or fan lands on the Page, control whether comments on posts are expanded by default, and limit what fans can post on the Page.

- **Mobile:** Mobile enables you to sign up to receive text messages from Facebook notifying you of activity on your Page. See Chapter 15 for more about Facebook Mobile.

- **Applications:** Below the main settings is a list of applications. You can adjust settings for these applications or delete applications altogether. For example, you can use the Links settings to specify whether fans can post links to the Page or only allow administrators to do so.

- **Admins:** To the right of Applications is a column that includes a section for admins (Page administrators). Here you control who, besides you, can administer the Page. Because most businesses and organizations have more than one person capable of managing their page, Facebook allows you to assign an unlimited number of admins. Admins, who access your Page through their personal accounts, remain anonymous to your Page's fans and can have their privileges revoked at any time by the person who created the Page.

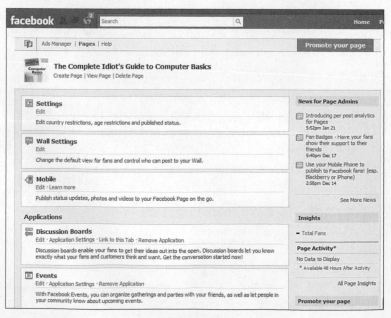

You can edit settings for your Page or its Wall and any applications you use on the page.

Publishing, Unpublishing, or Deleting Pages

If you edited your Settings and your Page is currently unpublished, you can still hold off on publishing your page until you read the following section on developing quality content, but why wait? You already have enough content to give visitors an inkling of what your Page is all about, and you can return at any time to flesh it out.

To publish your Page, pull it up as if you're going to edit it. (See more on getting back to your Page earlier in this chapter.) At the top of the right column of the page is a message indicating that your Page has not yet been published. In that message, click the **publish this Page** link.

You can always unpublish a Page without deleting it. Head to the Page and click **Edit Page** (below the photo). Click the **Edit** link in the Settings box, open the **Published** drop-down menu, click **Unpublished (visible to no one but admins),** and click **Save Changes.**

Assuming a Page has outlived its usefulness, you can delete it for good. Click **Advertising** (at the bottom of any Facebook screen), click the **Pages** tab, and, under the Page you want to delete, click **Delete Page.** When the confirmation dialog box pops up, click **Delete.**

You can publish your Page at any time.

Populating Your Page with Relevant and Compelling Content

Your Page is very similar to your Profile, complete with multiple tabs for posting status updates to the Wall, uploading photos, and hosting discussions. Use your Page accordingly to engage fans, keep them coming back for more, and inspire them to share your Page with their friends.

Engage is the key word here. This Page isn't as much about you, your business, or your products as it is about the topics your fans are interested in. We're not saying you should pander to the masses—that could turn fans off, too. You want to size up your audience and deliver the content they crave in a way that meets or exceeds their expectations. If you're in the restaurant biz, that may mean posting this week's specials. If you're promoting your band, it might mean posting lyrics or updates about the current tour. If you host a special event, you may want to gather fans for a group photo at the event and post the photo later. Treat your fans like friends instead of customers or clients, and you're likely to hit the bull's-eye.

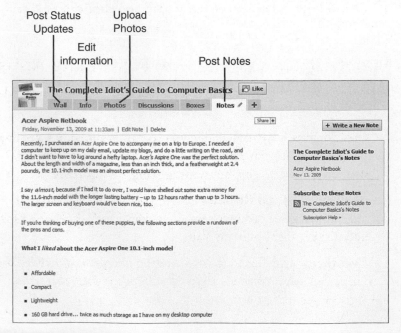

Use your Page to engage fans the same way you use your Profile to engage friends.

Resist the urge to post your product catalog. Far too many businesses treat social media, which is intended to be dynamic and interactive, as a shell for static web content. They essentially copy web content and post it on Facebook. This is ineffective and likely to do more harm than good.

Expanding Content with Other Facebook Apps

In addition to posting status updates and photos and facilitating discussions, consider using other Facebook applications to engage fans. You can use the Events app to announce special occasions, such as a grand opening, a conference, or a trade show. You can post a note to focus the spotlight on your "Fan of the Month" or announce the results of a recent contest. Use your imagination to think up clever uses for Facebook's standard apps.

FRIEND-LY ADVICE

To post events or apps, first create a tab for the app by clicking the tab with the + on it and selecting the desired app: Links, Events, Notes, or Video. If you just click Applications and then choose Events or Notes, the item will be posted to *your* Wall and won't be associated with the Page.

Accessorizing Your Page with Third-Party Apps

To further enhance your Page, you can add business apps from third-party developers. Following are some examples:

- **Promotions** for Pages enable you to run branded, interactive promotions on your Pages, including sweepstakes, contests, coupon giveaways, instant wins, gifting, and quizzes.

- **Testimonials** and **Reviews** enable you to collect customer testimonials and product/service reviews from Facebook fans and display them on your Page.

- **Eventbrite** provides tools for bringing people together for an event and selling tickets. If you're a budding rock star, this app could come in very handy.

- **Polls** make it easy to create online polls and analyze results with graphs that illustrate user responses across multiple demographics.

- **Marketplace** allows you to post images and descriptions of the items you or your business sell, along with job postings and more. (See Chapter 16 for more information.)

Feeding Your Blog to Your Facebook Business Page

If you or your organization already maintain a blog outside Facebook, manually posting content to your blog and then reposting it on Facebook is a waste of time. You can set up a feed on your Page that automatically pulls entries from your blog and displays them on your Facebook Page as notes. To set up an incoming blog feed, here's what you do:

1. Display the Page on which you want the feed to appear.

2. Click **Edit Page** (below the photo box). The Page settings appear.

3. Scroll down to the Applications section, and, in the Notes box, click **Edit.**

4. Under Notes Settings, click **Import a Blog.**

5. Click in the **Enter a website or RSS/Atom feed address** box and type the address of your blog or RSS or Atom feed, starting with **http://.**

6. Click the checkbox stating that you have the right to permit Facebook to reproduce the blog content on Facebook.

7. Click **Start Importing.** Assuming everything works according to plan, Facebook displays a preview of the imported blog.

8. Check the preview, and if it looks right, click **Confirm Import.** If it doesn't look right, or you just decide not to move forward with the import, click **Cancel.** Facebook returns you to the Notes page, on which you're likely to see at least one post from your blog (assuming you didn't cancel the operation).

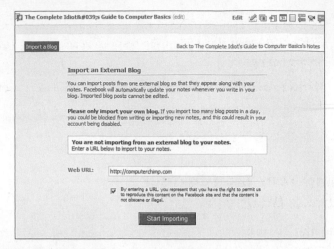

Set up a blog feed to pull posts from an existing blog and display them as notes.

Building and Maintaining Your Fan Base

"If you build it, they will come," is as untrue a statement on Facebook as it is throughout the rest of the web. Building, growing, and maintaining an active community of fans through a Facebook Page requires two key components:

- **A killer Page** with fresh, engaging, and interactive content.
- **Promotion.** Yep, that's right. You build a Page to promote something, and then you have to promote your Page. It never stops.

Facebook can't help you with the first component. It's entirely up to you to keep the content on your Page fresh and compelling and interact with fans regularly and in a meaningful way. Facebook does, however, provide you with several tools for promoting your page:

- **Become your own number one fan.** Pull up your Page and click the **Like** button (to the right of the Page title). Now at least your Page has one fan. When you become a fan, all your friends are notified via their News Feeds.

- **Invite your friends.** Click **Suggest to Friends** (below the Page's Profile picture) and send a message to the friends you think will be interested in the Page. Let them know about your new Page and ask them what they think of it.

- **Send updates to fans.** If you have something to offer that's really good, you can send an update to fans by clicking **Edit Page** (below the photo box) followed by **Send an Update to Fans** in the right column.

- **Link your Page to Twitter.** Twitter is a microblogging platform that is very popular. If you don't have a Twitter account yet, register for one at twitter.com and then edit your Page to link it to Twitter. The option should appear at the top of your Page. If it doesn't, click in the **Search** box (top menu), type **Twitter,** and press **Enter** to open the Twitter applications page.

- **Place a fan box or page badge on your website or blog.** A fan box can display a list of fans and streaming data from your Page as activity occurs on it. A page badge is smaller and can display the Page name, status, picture, and fans. To create a fan box or page badge, open your Page and click **Edit Page** (below the photo box), and then (off to the right below Promote your page) click **Promote with a Fan Box.** Click **Fan Box** or **Page Badges** and follow the instructions on the resulting screen to enter your preferences and choose the platform on which you want to post the badge. This displays a code you can copy and paste into your blog or website to display the object wherever you want it to appear.

- **Give your page its own vanity URL.** As soon as your Page has a certain number of fans (Facebook set the minimum at 25 last we checked), you can claim a vanity URL for your Page—a web address that more clearly and simply reflects the Page title. Go to Facebook.com/username, click **Set a user name** for your Pages (below the box that allows you to set a username for your profile), and follow the on-screen instructions.

Create a fan box to promote your Page through your website or blog.

POKE

Facebook is very particular about the way you promote your Page. Visit www.facebook.com/pages/manage/promo_guidelines.php, where you can find additional guidance on promoting your Facebook Page outside Facebook and a high-resolution "Find us on Facebook" badge suitable for displaying on your website or blog.

On the page where you can create a fan box or page badge, you may notice two other options: Widgets Home and Share. The Share option provides you with a code to paste on your website or blog allowing visitors to share your content with their friends on Facebook. The Widgets Home option takes you to a page with additional Facebook *widgets*.

DEFINITION

A **widget** (supposedly short for "windows gadget") is any object created by a third party that can be embedded on a web page.

Tracking Page Effectiveness with Page Insights

Wondering how many people visit your Page every day? The number and demographics of your Facebook fans and how frequently fans interact with your Page? Then pull up your Page Insights (Facebook's term for analytics). From your Home page, click **Ads and Pages** (left menu), and then click **View Page.** In the left column is a section with the title Insights, below which are statistics of recent Page activity. Click **See All** (below and off to the right of "Insights"). Page Insights provides additional statistics regarding fan interactions with your Page and fan demographics.

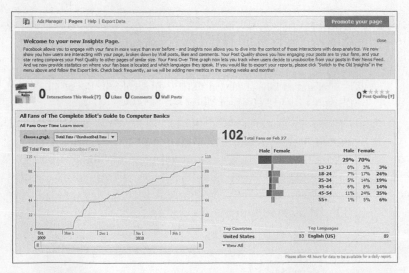

Page Insights present valuable statistics related to your Page.

To get the most out of your business activities on Facebook, you need to know what's working and what's not, which content your fans interact with most, and how fans interact with your brand and with one another. While you can glean some of this information from scanning each individual item on your Page's Wall, doing so is tedious and prone to miscalculation.

Enter Page Insights. From posting quality scores that measure how engaging your posts have been over a rolling seven-day period, to the number of fans interacting with your content and the number of interactions per post, Facebook provides the information you need to quickly evaluate the effectiveness of your efforts.

Facebook also e-mails you a weekly summary of your Insights, informing you of the number of fans you've gained (or lost) during the week; the number of Wall posts, Comments, and Likes; and the number of visits to the page. The message includes links to various Facebook features that can help you build your fan base.

The Least You Need to Know

- Businesses, organizations, and individuals interested in leveraging the power of online community should have a Page.
- This is social networking. It's not social selling. Use your Page to interact with customers and brand advocates as you would interact with colleagues and Facebook friends.
- To do anything related to Pages, scroll down to the footer, click **Advertising,** and click the **Pages** tab.
- Use all the tools in the shed to build your Page, including status updates, photos, notes, events, links, videos, discussions, and third-party apps.
- To build, maintain, and grow a fan base, keep your Page updated with clever, relevant content and promote the heck out of your Page.
- Cross-promote your Page and your website or blog by linking to your site from your Page and using badges or widgets to link your website or blog to Facebook.
- Use Page Insights to measure and monitor traffic, evaluate ROI, and identify obstacles to engagement.

Mastering the Soft Sell with Social Ads

In This Chapter

- Recognizing the potential of Facebook ads
- Using Facebook ads strategically in your marketing campaigns
- Doing the essential prep work
- Following Facebook's rules and regulations for posting ads
- Creating a Facebook ad that achieves your goals

Posting a standard advertisement on Facebook is like announcing a 75 percent off sale during the singing of "The Star-Spangled Banner." It'll earn you more enemies than friends. You need to carefully craft an ad that the Facebook community views as something worthy of its attention rather than as an intrusive billboard on the information superhighway.

In this chapter, we introduce you to the potential benefits (and a few drawbacks) of Facebook ads, step you through the process of developing an effective strategy, show you how to prepare your ad, and then assist you in launching and managing your advertising campaign.

Weighing the Pros and Cons of Facebook Ads

You can do a great deal of advertising on Facebook without spending a penny, so you may be wondering whether paid advertising is worth it. We can't answer that question for you, but we can provide you with the pros and cons to consider in making this decision for yourself.

> **FRIEND-LY ADVICE**
>
> Doing business on Facebook is more about relationship marketing than intrusion marketing. Don't expect to see a big boost in sales when you first start posting ads on Facebook. Consider using ads to develop a greater presence and following on Facebook by encouraging Facebook members to become fans of your page, join your brand-based group, or register for a special event.

Potential Benefits

When deciding where to invest your advertising budget, consider the following benefits of Facebook ads:

- **More than 400 million active members:** A lot of people spend a lot of time on Facebook—even more time than they spend watching TV, glancing at billboards, reading newspapers or magazines, or browsing the web. In other words, they're more likely to see an ad on Facebook than anywhere else.

- **Ability to target a specific demographic and locale:** Facebook enables you to target your ads by age, gender, education, geography, marital status, and more, so you stand to get more bang for your buck than with more generalized PPC (pay-per-click) advertising on the web. In addition, Facebook members are more motivated to provide accurate information about themselves and keep it up-to-date, meaning people are more likely to be who they say they are.

- **Ability to target keywords:** You can pack your ad with keywords to place your ad in front of Facebook members who express an interest in your products or services.

- **Potential bump from social interaction:** Your ad can include a call to action to do something on Facebook, such as become a fan or join a group. Whenever someone performs that call to action, it's likely to be posted to his Wall and News Feed where his friends can see it. This provides extra mileage for your ad.

- **Affordability and scalability:** You can spend as much or as little money per day as you like on your Facebook ads. Facebook can charge by impression or per click.

- **Ability to measure your ad's performance:** Facebook provides basic analytics so you can check your account for each ad's clicks, impressions, CPC (cost per click), and CPM (cost per thousand impressions ... the M stands for the "milli" in the metric system, not "millions").

Potential Drawbacks

Facebook ads may seem like the ideal solution for businesses or organizations of any size, but they're not without some potential drawbacks, including the following:

- **Lack of interest in ads:** People on Facebook gather to chat, not shop. Your ads are more like billboards or magazine advertisements that people may glance at in the midst of doing something else.

- **Poor timing versus search engine marketing:** When web users search on Google, Yahoo!, Bing, or other such sites, they're often trying to find a solution, product, or service. With search engine marketing, your ad catches them at the right time. This doesn't occur on Facebook and other social-media sites.

- **Lack of trust:** Facebook isn't very selective in determining who can advertise. As a result, many ads promote questionable products or services that turn off Facebook users to *all* ads.

Laying the Groundwork

You can slap together a Facebook ad in minutes, but before launching your first advertising campaign, spend some time brushing up on Facebook's rules and regulations, developing a strategy, and preparing the components of your ad—your message and graphic.

Brushing Up on Facebook Ads Rules and Regulations

To remain in good standing with Facebook, follow its rules. For an exhaustive (and exhausting) list of rules, head to www.facebook.com/ad_guidelines.php. The following list highlights the major do's and don'ts:

- No multiple accounts or automated creation of accounts for advertising purposes.

- No funny business on landing pages your ads link to, including pop-overs, pop-unders, fake close buttons, or bait-and-switch URLs (a link that makes visitors think they're going to a particular place but end up somewhere else).

- No using the Facebook name, brand, or logos in a way that even hints that Facebook endorses you, your company, or your products.

- No false, fraudulent, or deceptive ads.

- No lewd, crude, or otherwise inappropriate language or obscene, libelous, harassing, insulting, or unlawful content.

- No advertising firearms, illicit drugs, scams, get-rich-quick schemes, adult "friend finders," uncertified pharmaceutical products, nonaccredited colleges, or other goods or services that could be deemed dangerous, illegal, or of questionable value.

- Adhere to all of Facebook's privacy guidelines regarding member content.

- No spamming.

- Ads for alcoholic beverages or adult-related products or services must be age appropriate and not designed to lure minors.

- No copyright infringement.

- No using ads to trick users into downloading spyware or malware.

Setting a Measurable Goal

To determine how well any advertising campaign is performing, start with a measurable goal. With a Facebook ad, you typically want to set two measurable goals: one relating to traffic and the other to conversion rates. Specify how much traffic or what percentage increase in traffic from Facebook to your landing page or website you expect your ad campaign to generate. For conversion rates, specify the percentage of people who arrived from Facebook and then succeeded in performing the call to action included in the ad.

The goals you set are entirely up to you. You can set goals according to the number of visitors, percentage increase in visitors, cost per click, cost per click-through, or some other benchmark.

After setting one or more measurable goals, make sure you have the analytics in place to track each ad's success. Facebook can provide you with some statistics that apply directly to your ad, such as number of impressions or number of times an ad was clicked. To measure click-through or conversion rates, however, you must have analytics installed on your website or landing page. Google Analytics (www. google.com/analytics) is an excellent choice, and it's free!

The goal you set influences your strategy and the type of advertising you choose to do on Facebook:

- **Pay-per-click advertising:** When you're paying per click, targeting ads to the most appropriate demographic and geographical area is of prime importance. In addition, make sure your ad and landing page (a Facebook page or a page on your website) are well coordinated to encourage and facilitate your call to action.

- **Pay-per-view advertising:** When you're paying for impressions, brand identity is most important. The graphic you use should clearly communicate your brand or company, and the text should be clear and informative.

Targeting a Demographic and Locale

Make the most of the targeting features in Facebook ads. If you're running a local pizzeria, advertising to the entire country is probably a bad idea—especially if you're offering free delivery. You'll get more bang for your advertising buck by targeting a specific location. Likewise, if whatever you're advertising is more likely to appeal to a certain age group or gender, specify your target demographic when creating your ad.

Listing a Few Keywords

In search engine optimization (SEO), web developers use meta data such as page titles, page descriptions, and keywords to attract search engine attention and improve page rankings in search results. Keywords can play a similar role in Facebook ads—enabling Facebook to target specific ads to Facebook users who express an interest in a certain topic (by mentioning it in their Profiles, Wall posts, Notes, and even in their status updates).

Prior to creating an ad, invest some thought in which words and phrases Facebook members are likely to use in describing the product or service you're advertising. Sprinkle these keywords and phrases generously throughout your ad.

Settling on a Call to Action

Every ad, especially the pay-per-click variety, should include a call to action—a clear, direct message telling whoever is looking at the ad what to do. You don't want them to think—you tell them what to do. You usually want people to do two things: first, click on your ad, and then do something when they reach your website or landing page, such as register, order, shop, buy, obtain a quote, or check out special offers. These two goals should be well-coordinated; if your ad sets certain expectations, your website must meet or exceed those expectations and facilitate the visitor's ability to follow through on your call to action.

A call to action may also apply to activity within Facebook, such as becoming a fan, joining a brand-based group, or registering for an event.

Composing an Effective Message

In a Facebook ad, you don't have a lot of room to elaborate. You pretty much have to make your point in 25 words or fewer (25 characters for the title and 135 characters for the body). Use these words efficiently by composing a concise message that speaks clearly and directly to your audience. Here are some tips for creating quality ad copy:

- Be direct.

- Be clear.

- Keep it simple. Save the details for your website or landing page.

- Focus on the call to action.

- To reinforce brand identity, use your company or product name in the ad title or the body of the ad.

- Proofread the ad carefully before posting it. Nothing drives customers away more quickly than poor grammar and typos.

Finding Just the Right Picture

A high-quality image can catch the eye and reinforce the message your ad conveys. When selecting an image, make sure it's attractive and relevant to the product or service you're advertising.

The maximum size is 80 pixels tall by 110 pixels wide, which is pretty small. If your image contains text, don't expect it to be readable. The image should have an aspect ratio (height:width) of 4:3 or 16:9. Facebook resizes the image for you, if necessary, but for best quality, size it yourself before uploading it. No animated graphics or flash images are allowed.

Prior to posting a photo or image, open it in a photo-editing or graphics program and play around with the brightness, contrast, and color balance to achieve the highest quality possible. Photos in particular often appear too dark when displayed on a computer screen. (For more about image quality, see Chapter 7.)

Launching Your Advertising Campaign

After laying the groundwork, launching your ad campaign is a snap. All you need to do is transfer your text, upload an image, specify your targeted demographic, and choose a plan and pricing. The following sections step you through the process.

Creating Your Ad

To get started, scroll to the bottom of any Facebook page, click **Advertising**, and click **Create an Ad** (upper right). The Advertise on Facebook screen appears requesting the following four items:

- **Destination URL:** You have two options here. To link to a website or landing page outside Facebook, click in the **Destination URL** text box and type the page's web address (URL). If you have a page, group, event, or application on Facebook that you want to link to, click **I want to advertise something I have on Facebook,** and then select the item from the Facebook Content drop-down list. (This option is available only if you have a page, group, or event on Facebook.)

- **Title:** Type your ad title (up to 25 characters). If you're linking to something on Facebook, the title you already gave your page, group, or event appears in this box, and you're unable to edit it, which is good—you want it to be consistent.

- **Body Text:** Type the ad copy (up to 135 characters), being sure to include a clear call to action.

- **Image:** Click **Browse** and follow the on-screen cues to select and upload an image stored on your computer.

After entering all four items, click the **Continue** button. The Targeting options appear. You may need to scroll down to see them.

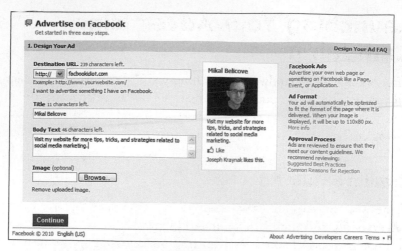

Create your Facebook ad.

Targeting Your Demographic

By default, Facebook targets your ad to a very broad demographic—Facebook members 18 years and older who live in the default location (for example, the United States). Facebook enables you to narrow your focus by location, age, gender, keywords, education, workplace, relationships, connections, and so on. Simply enter your preferences. As you change settings, Facebook displays (below the last setting) an estimate of the number of members that fit the targeted demographic.

When you're done, click the **Continue** button. The Campaigns and Pricing options appear.

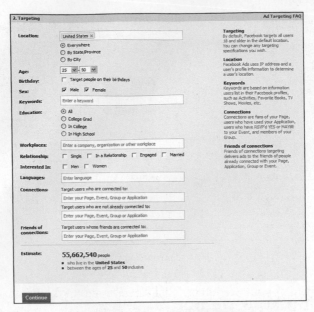

Target the desired demographic.

Choosing a Campaign and Pricing

After creating and targeting your ad, you must set up your ad campaign by entering your preferences for the following:

- **Account Currency:** U.S. dollars, euros, yen, whatever.

- **Campaign Name:** You can type a name for a new or existing campaign. Multiple ads in the same campaign share a daily budget and schedule.

- **Daily Budget:** The total amount you want to spend per day. The minimum is $1.

- **Schedule:** You can choose to have your ad run continuously starting today or between two specified dates and times.

- **Pay for Impressions or Clicks:** Choose to pay for impressions or clicks and specify a bid amount. Facebook suggests a bid amount, which you can raise or lower depending on the number of clicks or impressions you want to buy.

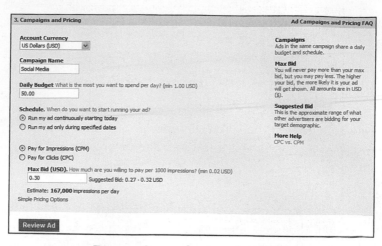

Enter preferences for your ad campaign.

After entering your preferences, click the **Review Ad** button. The Review Ad page appears, displaying your ad and details about your campaign.

Reviewing and Approving Your Ad

The Review Ad page shows you how your ad will appear in Facebook, provides details about the ad campaign, and prompts you to enter payment information. Carefully examine your ad and all details about it. You can make changes by clicking the **Edit Ad** link.

Review your ad and place your order.

After your ad passes inspection, enter payment information, and then click the **Place Order** button.

Monitoring and Fine-Tuning Your Campaign

Your ad campaign is up and running. Now you can kick back, cross your fingers, and hope it meets your goals, right? Not quite. You should keep tabs on your campaign and be prepared to make adjustments.

After a day or two, check your ad's click-through rate, along with its total clicks, impressions, and average CPC (cost per click) or CPM (cost per thousand impressions). To view these statistics, click **Advertising** (at the bottom of any Facebook page), and then click **or manage your existing ads** (upper right). From this page, you can click an ad to make changes to it.

If your ad is not quite meeting your expectations, consider making any of the following adjustments:

- Try a different call to action if Facebook members are not responding to your ad.

- Adjust your targeting preferences to be more restrictive if your conversion rate is low—your ad is getting plenty of impressions or clicks that are not translating into the desired activity.

- Adjust your targeting preferences to be less restrictive if your ad's impressions or clicks are too low.

- Try simplifying your ad.

- Try a different image.

The Least You Need to Know

- Use ads as a component of your relationship-marketing efforts on Facebook. Don't expect them to generate direct sales.

- Prior to creating an ad, set a clear goal so you can measure its success.

- Prepare your ad copy and image prior to creating an ad, so you're not just slapping something together at the last minute.

- To create an ad, click **Advertising** (at the bottom of any Facebook page), click **Create an Ad,** and follow the on-screen instructions.

- You can monitor and make changes to ads at any time. Click **Advertising** and then click **or manage your existing ads.**

Glossary

ad Short for *advertisement*, a paid promotion on Facebook that typically consists of an image, a small chunk of text, and a link, often displayed in the right column of most Facebook pages.

admin Short for *administrator*, a Facebook member who has greater access and authority to manage and configure a Group, Page, or other user-generated area on Facebook.

API Short for *application programming interface*, a set of programming instructions, procedures, and protocols accessible via the Internet that support the building of Applications on Facebook and other platforms.

app Short for *application*, a Facebook plugin that adds functionality to Facebook, such as enabling users to upload photos or videos and play games.

Chat A Facebook tool that enables friends to exchange text messages in real time.

comment A remark posted in response to an existing status update or other content, such as a Note, Photo, or Video.

developer Someone with programming skills who develops apps on Facebook.

Event A Facebook app that enables you to announce special occasions or gatherings, invite Facebook users to attend, and keep everyone you invited posted about any developments related to the happening.

Facebook   An online social network that enables friends, family members, colleagues, classmates, acquaintances, and businesses, brands, and organizations to get in touch and stay in touch with one another and meet others who may share their interests or experiences.

Facebook Connect   A feature that enables you to share your Facebook identity in other areas around the web, including your own website or blog.

fan   A Facebook member who chooses to follow another member's business- or organization-oriented page.

feed   A connection that pulls content from another source on the Internet and displays it on Facebook.

footer   The area at the bottom of every Facebook page containing links to Facebook Help, Advertising, Mobile, Careers, and other offerings.

friend list   A subset of friends that provides you with an easier way to follow and communicate only with that set of friends. Think of it as a clique.

friend request   A standardized message sent to another Facebook member whom you want to friend on Facebook.

friends   Any two people who mutually agree to officially connect with one another on Facebook.

Gift   A Facebook app that allows friends to exchange digital presents, which can sometimes be exchanged for real presents outside of Facebook.

Group   An area on Facebook where users with shared interests can gather. Groups can be exclusive or open to all.

left menu   The menu bar that runs along the left side of most Facebook pages and enables you to access the most frequently used Facebook features.

Like   A link you can click to indicate positive sentiment for something one of your friends or some other Facebook member has posted.

Marketplace   Facebook classified ads application, powered by Oodle.

member   Anyone with a Facebook account.

messages   E-mail communiqués sent internally via Facebook to other Facebook members.

Mobile   A Facebook app that enables you to log in to your Facebook account and use Facebook from a cell phone or other portable communications device.

network   An offline community of people related by locale or experience, such as a town, school, or place of employment.

News Feed   One of the main areas on Facebook, which displays activities your friends have chosen to share with you.

Notes   A core Facebook app that enables you to post longer entries than you'd normally post in a status update and provides a way to feed your blog (if you have one) into your Facebook Profile.

notification   A message Facebook sends you and/or displays on the notification list to let you know when something of importance has occurred, such as someone commenting on your status update or the receipt of a message.

officer   A Facebook user in a Group who holds a special status but does not have the privileges to configure or manage the group as an admin (see *admin*).

page   A page on Facebook that's typically used to promote a business, organization, product, or brand.

Photos   A core Facebook app that enables you to upload digital photographs to your account and create, manage, and share photo galleries.

Poke   A Facebook feature that enables you to let a friend know, in real time, that you're thinking about him or her.

Profile   A collection of information a Facebook member enters about herself along with an optional photo.

Profile tabs   Clickable labels on a Facebook member's Home page or a business-based page or group for accessing specific data, including the Wall, photos, or notes.

Publisher   The tool for posting Facebook status updates to a Wall or the News Feed.

RSS feed   See *feed*.

SMS   Acronym for Short Message Service, a technology that enables the exchange of text messages using a cell phone or other mobile communications device. Through the magic of SMS, you can also post content to Facebook using a mobile phone.

status update   A microblogging tool on Facebook that enables members to post brief messages, typically to share observations, insights, and experiences.

tag   To label yourself or a friend in a Photo, Video, Note, or other item posted on Facebook. When you tag someone else, Facebook sends the person a notification.

top menu   The blue bar that appears at the top of every Facebook page, which enables you to access the most frequently used areas on Facebook.

Video   A core Facebook app that enables users to upload and share video clips.

Wall   A quieter area on Facebook where you and your friends can post status updates, comments, photos, video clips, links, and more. While the News Feed displays all activity, the Wall filters out a lot of stuff to focus more on your recent activity and what you and your friends specifically post on one another's Walls.

Wall-to-Wall   A conversation carried on between two friends posting to one another's Walls.

Index